SEP   2016

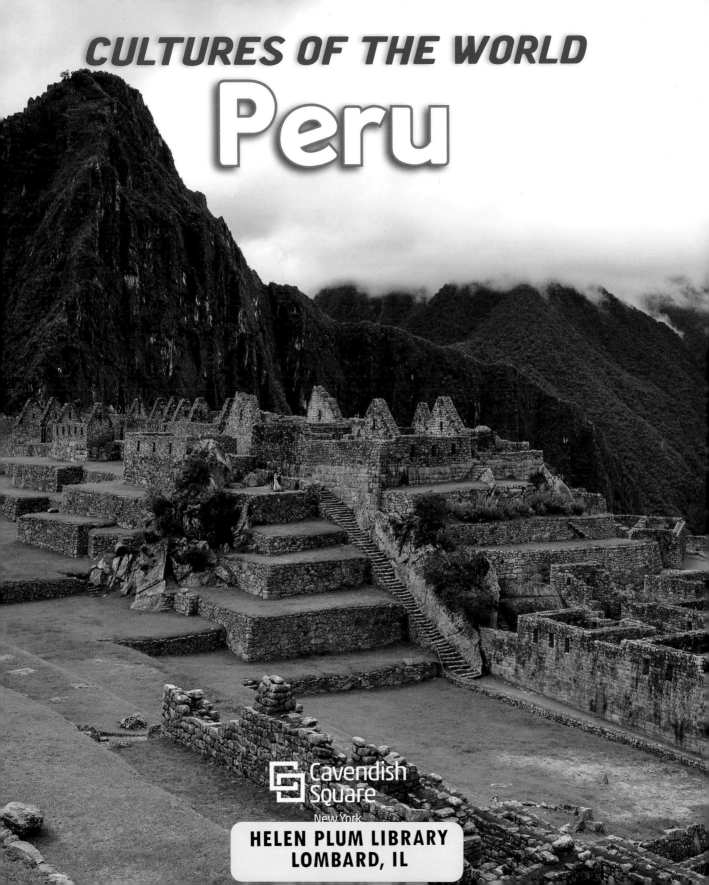

CULTURES OF THE WORLD
Peru

Cavendish Square
New York

Published in 2017 by Cavendish Square Publishing, LLC
243 5th Avenue, Suite 136, New York, NY 10016
Copyright © 2017 by Cavendish Square Publishing, LLC

Third Edition

Library of Congress Cataloging-in-Publication Data

Names: Falconer, Kieran, 1970- author. | Quek, Lynette, author. | Nevins, Debbie, author.
Title: Peru / Kieran Falconer, Lynette Quek, and Debbie Nevins.
Description: New York : Cavendish Square Publishing, [2016] | Series: Cultures of the world | Includes bibliographical references and index.
Identifiers: LCCN 2016008998 (print) | LCCN 2016009199 (ebook) | ISBN 9781502618436 (library bound) | ISBN 9781502618443 (ebook)
Subjects: LCSH: Peru--Juvenile literature.
Classification: LCC F3408.5 .F35 2016 (print) | LCC F3408.5 (ebook) | DDC 985--dc23
LC record available at http://lccn.loc.gov/2016008998

Writers: Kieran Falconer, Lynette Quek; Debbie Nevins, third edition
Editorial Director, third edition: David McNamara
Editor, third edition: Debbie Nevins
Art Director, third edition: Jeffrey Talbot
Designer, third edition: Jessica Nevins
Production Assistant, third edition: Karol Szymczuk
Cover Picture Researcher: Jeffrey Talbot
Picture Researcher, third edition: Jessica Nevins

PICTURE CREDITS

PRECEDING PAGE
The splendor of Machu Picchu

Printed in the United States of America

CONTENTS

PERU TODAY

PERU IS A LAND OF EXTRAORDINARY BEAUTY, CONTRAST, AND complexity. Here, the landscape sweeps from barren deserts to the cloud-piercing peaks of the Andes, across vast plateaus and giant canyons, then suddenly plunges into steep valleys of green. The Pacific Ocean laps at the country's long, dry coast on the west of the South American continent, while the Amazon River snakes through its immense jungle interior. That lush, dense jungle is home to the greatest diversity of plants and animals on the planet, as well as some of the few remaining human outposts untouched by modernity.

This is a country whose past is still very much present in ways that are at once deeply wonderful—and yet worrisome. The "wonderful" is easy to find; it attracts more than three million tourists each year. From the enigmatic "Lost City" of Machu Picchu high in the mountains to the mysterious Nazca Lines etched on the coastal desert, the land evokes the mysticism and awe of past civilizations.

Archaeologists continue to make new discoveries. In 2015, they unearthed the remains of a 3,500-year-old woman from the El Paraíso archaeological site just north of Lima. The colonial past is evident in the gorgeous Spanish architecture

Peruvian chef Gaston Acurio looks on in a kitchen in Lima.

of Lima and Arequipa, while Cuzco, the ancient capital of the Inca Empire, offers Incan temples and Baroque cathedrals alike. Magnificent festivals, with a mix of Catholic and Incan motifs, are testaments to cultural adaptation, seasoned with Spanish, indigenous, African, and Asian influences.

Those "seasonings" are especially noticeable in Peruvian cuisine, which is often heralded as "the best in the South America." Indeed, Peru's capital Lima was the only city in Latin America chosen as one of ten top gastronomic destinations, according to *National Geographic*'s "Where to Travel for Food in 2016." With his fresh interpretations of Peruvian flavors, the star chef, TV personality, and restaurateur Gaston Acurio is partly responsible for thrusting Peruvian cuisine into the stratosphere of international fine dining. However, the country's unique "fusion cuisine" has a long history, which has stewed and simmered for centuries in the multicultural pot that is Peru.

One of the great contributing factors to the food scene is the quality of the food itself. With twenty-eight climates, Peru grows a bounty of native fruits and vegetables that folks in other parts of the world can only dream of: cacao fruit, lúcuma, aguaymanto, pepino, camu camu, and noni, just to name a few—not to mention more than three thousand varieties of potato.

On the other hand, Peru is also an important and growing exporter. Thanks to asparagus, grapes, avocados, and mangoes, Peru is the world's eighth largest fruit and vegetable producer. The United States is the leading market for Peru's berry exports. US shoppers looking for fresh berries off season stand a good chance of finding Peruvian fruit in their local grocery store. In 2015, blueberry exports from La Libertad—which grows 90 percent of Peru's blueberries—amounted to over $76 million. That represents a 236 percent increase over exports in 2014.

A variety of fresh tropical fruits attracts buyers in an outdoor market.

With beautiful scenery, great food, a vibrant culture, and a deep connection to their past, one might conclude that Peruvians must be very happy people—if such a thing can be determined. In fact, certain organizations *do* quantify how happy, in general, different populations of people are, from one country to the next. These organizations, which include the United Nations Development Program, evaluate various quality-of-life indicators, including life expectancy, education, safety, and per capita income, to create a composite statistic for purposes of ranking. Some groups also consider subjective indicators, such as perceptions of government corruption, community and emotional support, freedom to make choices, and overall feelings of life satisfaction. The researchers use the results to compare one country to another and also to track a country's progress, or lack of, over time.

The 2015 Human Development Index (HDI), issued by the UN, ranked Peru as number 84 in the world out of 188 countries, with Norway being number 1 and Niger number 188. Other groups place Peru somewhere in the

People stroll along the Jirón de la Unión, a pedestrian boulevard in the historic center of Lima.

middle as well. The Legatum Prosperity Index finds Peru to be number 82 of 162 nations. The 2014 Gallup-Healthways State of Global Well-Being put Peru at 91 out of 145.

Statistics are cold and hard, however, and only paint a general impression of a county's well being. Peru may not be the happiest place on earth, statistically, but it's far from the worst. Nevertheless, like any nation, it has its problems. For decades, Peru has been struggling to come to terms with the darker parts of its past. In the 1980s and 1990s, the "dirty war" between the government's corrupt leaders and the Shining Path guerrilla rebels caused a great deal of bloodshed, fear, and misery.

Those matters remain unsettled as fallout from those years affects current events today. As the nation headed into the 2016 presidential election, for example, political figures from the bad old days were in the running, either directly or implicitly. Presidential candidates included Javier Velasco, son of the former dictator Juan Velasco Alvarado. There was also Keiko Fujimori, daughter of Alberto Fujimori, the former president imprisoned for crimes against humanity and corruption. Alan Garcia, a two-time former president, was also a candidate. He is credited with overseeing great economic growth during his second term, 2006 to 2011. However, he is also accused of allegedly selling presidential pardons to drug traffickers for $150,000 each, when, at the end of his second administration, he reportedly pardoned some four hundred convicted drug traffickers. Also in the running was General Daniel Urresti, who was simultaneously being investigated on allegations of ordering the assassination of journalist Hugo Bustíos in 1988. (Reportedly, more than fifty journalists have been murdered in Peru since 1980, and almost none of those cases have been prosecuted.)

Even as Peru functions as a modern democracy, its government remains tarnished and unsteady. For as well as Peru's economy has been doing, people wonder if its shadow economy—that is, its illicit economy—is what's really driving the country. In recent years, Peru and its neighbor Colombia have been sharing the dubious distinction of being the world's top cocaine producers. According to the UN, Peru topped Colombia in 2013, but was bumped back to second place again in 2015.

Analysts worry that Peru is becoming a narco state—that is, a state whose economy depends heavily on narcotics and other drugs. Typically, the most powerful people in the illicit drug trade have strong political influence. The weaker a national government is, the more likely it is that drug lords and kingpins will flex their muscle. Observers who are already concerned about the growing role of cocaine cash in Peru's public institutions are doubtful that any of the 2016 presidential frontrunners—especially those with past government experience—have the will to tackle the problem. The concern is troubling, because this beautiful country's future hangs in the balance.

Just a month before the April 10, 2016 presidential election, Peru's electoral tribunal barred candidate Julio Guzmán from the race due to a technical error in the registration of his candidacy. Guzmán, an economist, was running second to Keiko Fujimori, and posed the closest threat to her election. Many critics called the decision a sign of fraud and corruption in Peru's government,

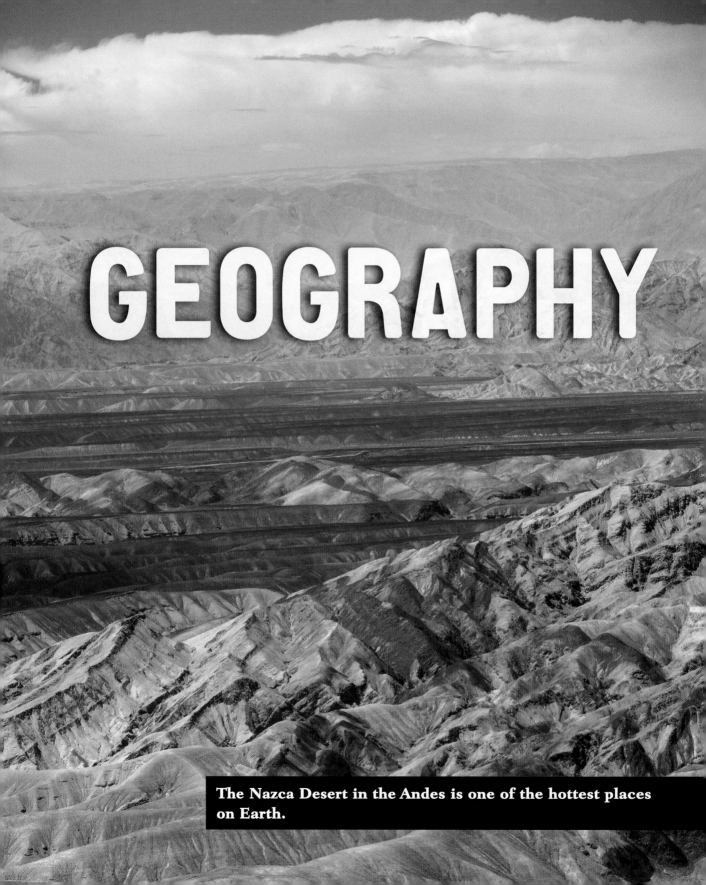

GEOGRAPHY

The Nazca Desert in the Andes is one of the hottest places on Earth.

1

PERU IS A COASTAL COUNTRY ON the Pacific Ocean side of the South American continent. With 1,500 miles (2,500 kilometers) of coast, its beaches are well known as a surfer's paradise. Peru is also a mountainous country that boasts the world's second-highest mountain range and two deepest canyons. Moreover, Peru is a jungle country that extends deep into the Amazon. About 60 percent of the country is covered by dense rain forest—only 5 percent of the people live in that part of Peru.

Peru has an area of 496,222 square miles (1,285,215 sq km)—almost the size of Alaska. In the west, its coastline is one of the driest in the world, and in the east, its Amazon rain forest is warm and humid. The Andes form the country's backbone, and have the coldest temperatures; and the Colca Canyon is twice as deep as the Grand Canyon. Lake Titicaca is the world's highest navigable lake.

Yes, this is a country of widely varied terrain and an astonishing range of geographic extremes. Peru is the third largest country in South America, after Brazil and Argentina, and has the fifth largest population. It is a tropical country with its northern tip nearly touching the Equator.

Peru is home to the *Puya raimondii*, the world's tallest flowering plant. It grows a spike more than 30 feet (9 meters) tall and only grows in the Andes at elevations above 10,000 feet (3,000 meters). A bromeliad, it takes decades, and sometimes more than a century, to bloom. Then it produces thousands of white flowers resembling lilies. As if that isn't dramatic enough, the plant blooms only once and then dies.

The terrain presents formidable difficulties to Peru's human inhabitants and especially to the farmers, who are at the mercy of a climate that varies from very hot to very cold. It has also been a great obstacle in unifying the nation, separating the mestizo-Hispanic people of the coast, the indigenous Andean people of the highlands, and those of the Amazon Basin. Only recently have roads been built to link remote areas with the rest of the country.

GEOGRAPHIC REGIONS

Peru consists of three main areas: the Costa, or western coast along the Pacific Ocean; the Selva, the rain forests of the Amazon Basin to the east of the Andes; and the Sierra, or central Andes highlands and mountains.

THE COAST Made up of deserts, plains, beaches, and valleys, the Costa lies between the Pacific Ocean on the west and the Andes on the east. It varies in width from about 10 to 100 miles (16 to 160 km) and covers just over 10 percent of the country. The Costa has become the most densely populated

Lima, Peru, is situated on the Pacific Coast.

part of Peru because Lima, the capital, is located there. This small region has attracted nearly half the population of Peru because it offers a higher standard of living, more employment opportunities, and a well developed infrastructure.

Even though the Costa lies beside the ocean, the region is extremely dry and cool, with long stretches of arid plains. The main reason for this is the cold Humboldt Current, which flows from the Antarctic, producing sea fogs but little rain. More than three hundred species of fish thrive off the coast, turning the area into a fishing paradise and Peru into one of the world's leading producers of fish. To the north is the mineral-rich Sechura Desert.

A child stands in a canoe in Santa Rita, a community deep inside the Amazon rain forest.

THE JUNGLE The Selva (meaning "jungle") covers mountain slopes to the east of the Andes (the area is sometimes called the Montaña). It makes up the part of the Amazon Basin that lies in Peru. It occupies nearly two-thirds of the country's territory, and is home to Peru's largest nature reserves. Covered with lush vegetation, the jungle grows more profuse and dense as one ventures eastward. Over 70 percent of the planet's flora and fauna can be found there.

Hundreds of rivers and streams penetrate the jungle, and its inhabitants, including native tribes, settle along the waterways. Rivers are the main highways because roads are quickly destroyed or overgrown. Navigation is hazardous and the water sometimes shallow, but the tribes rely on these rivers as a means to ship local produce, wood, and animals. The area is rich in timber, rubber, coffee, tropical fruit, and medicinal plants. Besides natural gas, 80 percent of Peru's oil reserves are located in this region, and their quantities are sufficient to cover the energy needs of Lima.

Mountains slope down to a green valley.

THE MOUNTAINS The Andes mountain chain is the longest continuous range in the world, extending more than 4,500 miles (7,240 km) along the western side of South America and passing through many countries from the Isthmus of Panama in the north to Tierra del Fuego in the south. The Peruvian Central Andes, or *Sierra*, divides the dry coastal region from the tropical Amazon jungle in the east. The Sierra covers a quarter of Peru's surface at an average height of 12,000 feet (3,660 m). It includes the *Altiplano*, or high plain, that runs through southern Peru and into Bolivia.

The highest mountains in this region are the snowcapped Yerupaja at 21,500 feet (6,550 m) and the Huascarán at 22,205 feet (6,765 m). The Huascarán is the second highest peak in South America and the fourth highest in the Western Hemisphere. The climate of the Sierra is as varied as the landscape. At higher altitudes it can be freezing in any month of the year, but it also gets hotter than at the Equator.

There are also many extinct and semi-extinct volcanoes in the southern part of the highlands. These cone-shaped volcanoes continue southward down the western side of Lake Titicaca and along the border with Chile and Bolivia. Near the city of Arequipa, the active El Mistí volcano, at 18,000 feet (5,486 m), is the third largest in South America.

The word *andes* is thought to have come from the Incan word *andenes*, which refers to the terraces built by the Incas to level land that was too steep to be irrigated. This terracing system of agriculture enabled large areas of hilly terrain to be cultivated and is still employed in some areas. Although at first they may appear inhospitable to both habitation and farming, over half the world's agricultural specimens are cultivated there.

More people live in the Andes than in any other large highland region in the world. Until recently, a majority of Peruvians lived in the Sierra. Today 36 percent of the population lives there. Because of the high altitude, the air is very thin, and many new visitors are affected by *soroche* (SAW-roche), or altitude sickness, which produces a feeling of nausea. The local people have adapted to the altitude over generations by developing thick chests and large lungs to efficiently draw the limited oxygen from the air.

Inca ruins in Peru's Sacred Valley include this terraced landscape in the village of Pisac.

Llamas are native to Peru and have been domesticated since prehistoric times. The Incas used them extensively. Llamas were used to carry burdens, such as food supplies, and for sacrifice in religious ceremonies; their wool and hide were used in clothing and their dung for fuel.

Llamas are useful in the difficult Andean terrain because of their high tolerance for thirst, their endurance, and their ability to subsist on a wide variety of forage. However, when llamas are overloaded or exhausted, they will lie down, hiss, spit, and kick, and refuse to move until they are relieved of some of the weight or until they are rested enough to continue the journey.

The llama's head resembles a camel's, with large eyes, a split nose, a harelip, and no upper teeth. Llamas range in color from the common pure white to black, with mixtures of black, brown, and white in between. Their wool is used for blankets and clothing.

LAKES AND RIVERS

Lake Titicaca has been a population center since before the time of the Incas. At around 350 miles (560 km) in length and 100 miles (160 km) in width, Titicaca is so large it has waves like the sea and contains more than thirty islands. Titicaca is divided between Peru and its neighbor Bolivia and serves as Peru's main trade route with Bolivia. It lies at an elevation of 12,500 feet (3,810 m), making it the world's highest navigable body of water.

Other natural trade routes include the many rivers that run through the Selva, some of them tributaries of the Amazon. The Marañón and Ucayali

Rivers begin 17,200 feet (5,240 m) up in Peru's Andes, merging near Nauta to form the mighty Amazon River, which then gradually plunges down waterfalls to the tropical rain forests that line most of the 2,200 miles (3,540 km) the river travels en route to the Atlantic Ocean.

CITIES

Most of Peru's large cities are located in the coastal area. As Peru's commercial and educational center, Lima and the port at Callao contain over a third of Peru's population. Almost 70 percent of the nation's economic activities are conducted there. It was founded in 1535 by Spanish conquistador Francisco Pizarro, who called it Ciudad de los Reyes, "City of Kings." Other large cities in the Costa include Trujillo, a commercial and industrial center, Chiclayo, and Chimbote.

Trujillo, in coastal northwestern Peru, is the country's second most populous city.

Most cities in the Andes are small. The largest is Arequipa, a major wool market with about 862,000 inhabitants. It serves as the seat of the Constitutional Court of Peru. Cuzco, located high in the Andes, has about 435,000 people and is the ancient Incan capital.

The main town in the lowland jungle region is Iquitos, a bustling port city. Located on the banks of the Amazon River, it has about 500,000 inhabitants. Although only 600 miles (965 km) from Lima, Iquitos was so inaccessible before the advent of air travel that to get there from Lima required making a 7,000-mile (11,265 km) journey via the Pacific and through the Panama Canal to the Amazon.

FLORA AND FAUNA

Peru is teeming with wildlife. It has more than 1,800 species of birds. The waters off the coast hold an abundant and diverse sea life, and along the shore vast numbers of seabirds come to feed on the ocean creatures.

An Andean condor soars against the blue sky.

Farther inland, the most celebrated Peruvian bird is the condor, a rare but beautiful sight in the Andes. It is a large black bird with a white ruff and a wingspan of up to 10 feet (3 m). As a member of the vulture family, the condor usually feeds on dead animals, but it will sometimes kill its prey. It is not, however, a hunter and is unable to grasp or carry prey because its feet are similar to those of a chicken.

In the Andes, an equally iconic Peruvian animal, the llama, was used for centuries as a pack animal before horses and donkeys were introduced. The Spanish brought many new animals to South America. Horses, cows, pigs, chickens, and cattle, none native to Peru, flourished when introduced. The Andes are also home to the puma or mountain lion. The Incas revered the puma as a symbol of power and elegance, but it has suffered recently from indiscriminate hunting. Deer are also common, as is the Andean fox, which frequently raids both sheep herds and garbage cans.

The lowland jungle has many different types of wildlife, including tapirs, jaguars, snakes, monkeys, colorful parrots, alligators, and flesh-eating piranhas. It has been little influenced by humans until recently. Its botanical diversity consists of an average of five hundred different tree species per square mile. Tropical rain forests are the oldest continuous terrestrial habitat on earth, so plants have had a much longer time to evolve into different species than in other areas. Although tropical rain forests presently cover less than 2 percent of the Earth's surface, or 6 percent of its land mass, they are home to more than 50 percent of all plant and animal species on the planet.

But these animals and, especially, the Amazonian flora are all in danger of possible extinction due to development. Although tropical rain forests have been around for millions of years, they have been on the decline during the last century. This is in direct relation to growth in the human population. According to the Rainforest Action Network, if destruction continues at the present rate, most of the remaining rain forests will be gone by the year 2060. Although they look lush and healthy, these ecosystems are extremely fragile, and if cleared for farmland, the soil rarely provides enough nutrients to sustain crops for more than five years. Conservation has become essentially vital. Peru now has about 15 percent of its land protected by a system of national parks, reserves, and sanctuaries. Conservation groups have also proliferated in recent years.

A jaguar is at home in the jungle.

INTERNET LINKS

www.discover-peru.org/category/geography
This site has numerous articles about Peruvian geography, wildlife and cities.

www.livescience.com/27897-andes-mountains.html
This is a quick overview of the geography of the Andes Mountains.

www.lonelyplanet.com/peru/amazon-basin
The Amazon Basin region is highlighted on this site, with various articles and photos.

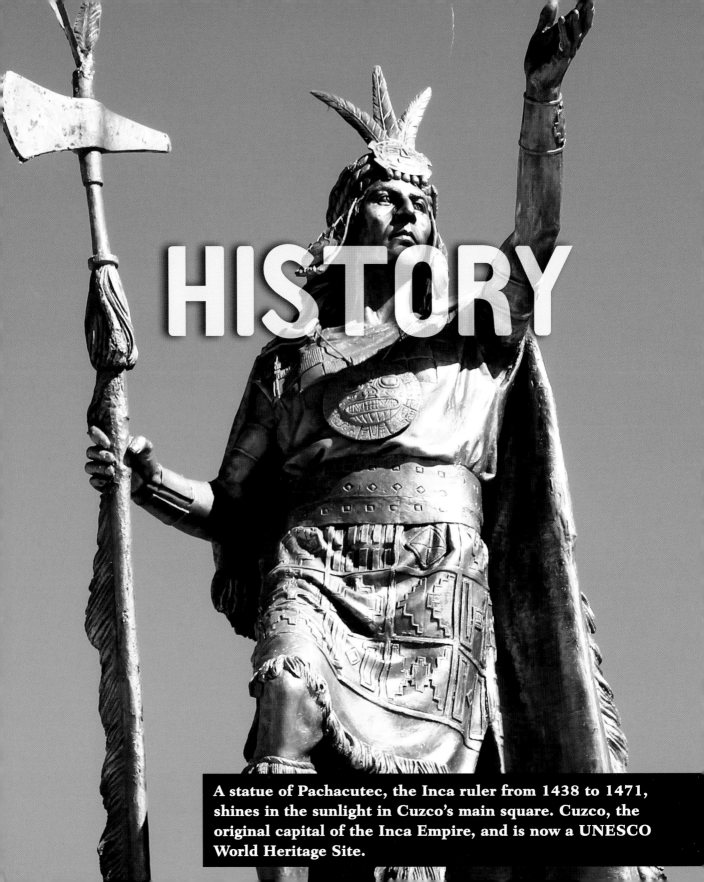

HISTORY

A statue of Pachacutec, the Inca ruler from 1438 to 1471, shines in the sunlight in Cuzco's main square. Cuzco, the original capital of the Inca Empire, and is now a UNESCO World Heritage Site.

2

PERU HAS UNDERGONE MANY changes in its history but has never lost its Incan character. The Incan civilization was the greatest South American empire ever known, even today.

Peru has been ruled by a diverse range of peoples, from the nomadic tribes of the prehistoric period to the city-states from which the Incan empire developed.

The Peruvian republic has been in existence for almost two hundred years. For three hundred years before that, Peru was under Spanish colonial rule. Spanish domination was followed by self-government,

The ancient Inca city of Machu Picchu sits high up in the mountains.

"When has it ever happened, either in ancient or modern times, that such amazing exploits have been achieved? Over so many climes, across so many seas, over such distances by land, to subdue the unseen and unknown? Whose deeds can be compared with those of Spain? Not even the ancient Greeks and Romans."
—Francisco Xerez (1495-1565), secretary to Francisco Pizarro, in his book, *Reports on the Discovery of Peru*

but foreign interests continued to dominate the country. Oligarchy (government by the few), dictatorship, and military coups have plagued its history.

BEGINNINGS

Peru's first inhabitants were nomadic tribes that probably migrated from Asia and moved into South America over successive generations. Around 5000 BCE communities began to develop, supported by a growth in agriculture. Corn, gourds, and cotton were cultivated in irrigated fields, and the population began to mushroom.

The Chavíns first united people into a distinct cultural group around 1000 BCE. The Mochica and Nazca cultures dominated Peru from 200 CE to 1100 CE. Intertribal warfare meant that no empire could last long or extend very far. These cultures were skilled at producing fine ceramics and elaborate metalwork and at weaving complex designs. The Incan culture, beginning around 1200 CE, derived much from these tribes' art and architecture while establishing the primacy of the sun cult and the Quechua language.

The Tello Obelisk at the Chavín de Huántar archaeological site in the Andean highlands dates to about 900 BCE.

THE INCAS

The Incas were originally a small tribe, one of many, whose domain did not extend very far from their capital, Cuzco. They were almost constantly at war with neighboring tribes. Around the year 1200 they began to expand their realm. Their legends do not predate this time.

The Incan empire expanded rapidly with the reign of the ninth emperor, Pachacútec, from 1438 to 1471. This period marked the start of reliable historical records, and differed from earlier times when rulers were considered to be almost mythic. Pachacútec was the most innovative and important of the Incan emperors and is said to have designed and built Cuzco. His first conquest came when his father, Viracocha, placed him in

MACHU PICCHU: THE REMAINS OF A CIVILIZATION

Yale University archaeologist Hiram Bingham rediscovered the "lost city" of Machu Picchu in 1911. Built on a mountaintop more than five hundred years ago by the Incas, the ruins are a complex of temples, palaces, and observatories standing 8,000 feet (2,440 m) above sea level. Little is known of the site, for the Incas left no records and the Spanish conquistadors never discovered it. Archaeologists believe the city could have been a religious or ceremonial sanctuary, because of the excavation of 173 Incan tombs.

Whatever its origins, the site is an astonishing tribute to the architectural skill of the Incas. Situated in a depression high above the Urubamba Valley, these remarkably intact ruins include baths, houses, even cemeteries, all surrounded by terracing on the mountainsides designed to provide food for the residents. Gradually, other ruins in the area are being excavated, which may help unravel the enigma of Machu Picchu.

The site was added to the UNESCO World Heritage List in 1983. It has become Peru's top tourist attraction and major revenue generator, attracting more than four hundred thousand visitors each year.

charge of the defense of Cuzco against the neighboring Chancas. Not only did he defend the city, but he also overwhelmingly defeated the Chancas, one of the most powerful confederations in the area. This was the start of a mighty Incan conquest.

From 1463 to 1493, Pachacútec and his son Topa Inca (Emperor Topa) expanded the territory north to the present-day border with Colombia

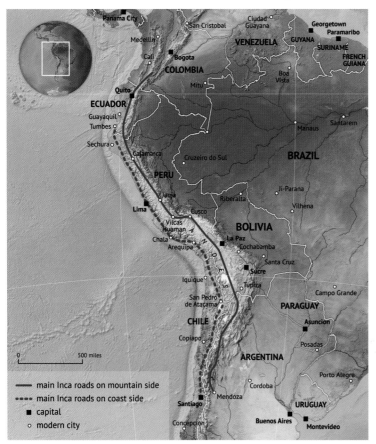

In 2014, the Inca road system, shown on this map, became a UNESCO World Heritage Site.

Map legend:
— main Inca roads on mountain side
···· main Inca roads on coast side
■ capital
○ modern city

0   500 miles

and Ecuador and south as far as Chile. The newly acquired coastline extended 2,500 miles (4,000 km) and encompassed 380,000 square miles (984,200 sq km) of territory with a population of around 16 million.

This huge realm was linked by a remarkable road system and was administered through a complex bureaucracy that divided labor and land among the state, the gods, and the *ayllus* (EYE-yoos), or villages. The empire initiated a massive program of agricultural terracing to maximize land use, and also started the construction of palaces and temples.

CIVIL WAR

By the end of the fifteenth century the Incan empire was beginning to suffer from overexpansion. The emperor Huayna Capac created a new Incan city, Quito, the capital of present-day Ecuador. Preferring this city to the traditional Incan center of Cuzco, he ruled the empire from Quito with his favorite son, Atahualpa, and installed his older son, Huáscar, at Cuzco. In the last year of his life he tried to arrange the division of the empire to ensure that Atahualpa retained Quito, but this was rejected by Huáscar, the legitimate heir who was backed by many Cuzco priests and nobles.

With the sudden death of Huayna Capac in 1527, civil war broke out. Atahualpa, backed by his father's army, was more powerful than Huáscar, and in two major victories defeated his half-brother. At the end of the last battle, in 1532, Atahualpa withdrew with his army to the hot baths of Cajamarca in the north of the country. There he soon began hearing strange tales of travelers from afar journeying to meet him.

THE CONQUEST OF THE INCAS

Spanish interest in Peru began with the discovery of the Pacific Ocean in 1513. Tales about the riches inland led Francisco Pizarro, a Spanish soldier, in search of El Dorado, the mythical City of Gold. In 1528 Pizarro, returning from an expedition to the Caribbean, sought the authority of King Charles V of Spain to conquer the new territory. In 1532, with fewer than 180 Spanish adventurers, Pizarro arrived on Peru's northern coast.

Pizarro and his men set out to make contact with Atahualpa, who had just retired victorious from battle and was resting at Cajamarca with an army of thirty thousand. Pizarro sent a message asking Atahualpa to come and see him. Because Atahualpa was emperor, it was deemed respectful that Pizarro should go to see *him* instead. But Atahualpa made the trip himself, curious to know more about these strange people. He had an entourage of more than five thousand and did not believe he could possibly be harmed. Although heavily outnumbered, the Spanish had the advantage of surprise. The Spanish also had guns, cannons, horses (which the Incas had never seen before), armor, and chain mail, which made the Incan wooden weapons useless. As a result, most of the Incas were killed, and Atahualpa was taken captive.

Pizarro's capture of Atahualpa and demand for ransom sent the empire into confusion. The wounds had barely healed from the bitter civil war, and now the state was again leaderless. Atahualpa agreed to pay the ransom by filling one room full of gold and another smaller room twice with silver. Incredulous, the Spanish agreed. Within six months a room 22 by 18 feet (7 by 6 meters) was filled with gold to a height of 9 feet (3 m). Gold and silver had been ordered from every corner of the empire, enough to make all the men very wealthy, but Pizarro had no intention of keeping his promise. Meanwhile, Atahualpa had been sending secret messages to his nobles in Cuzco. Believing that Huáscar was in league with the Spanish, he ordered

A statue of Francisco Pizarro stands in Lima.

An old print illustrates the execution of the last Inca, emperor Atahualpo, in 1533.

Huáscar's death. Pizarro's captains became worried by such maneuvers and, pressuring Pizarro, brought Atahualpa to trial in July 1533, where he was baptized as a Christian and then killed.

In November 1533 Pizarro went to Cuzco, where he appointed a puppet emperor, Manco Inca Yupanqui, to control the populace. Thus began nearly three centuries of colonial rule. Manco Inca Yupanqui, for his part, was not content to be a puppet to the conquerors. A virtual prisoner of the Spanish in Cuzco, he escaped in 1536, raised an army, and besieged Spanish strongholds. He was defeated in 1537 and retreated to the mountains, where he waged guerrilla warfare until his assassination in 1544.

Pizarro founded Lima in 1535, as it made a better transportation center than Cuzco. Wealth was brought to Lima from all over the country and then shipped to Spain. In the various regions of Peru, Spanish *encomenderos* (en-koh-men-DER-ohs), or local agents, exacted taxes from villages. For most of the natives, there was no real difference between their old Incan over-lords' exploiting them and the Spanish. The natives had had little chance to identify with the Incan rulers because of the distance they kept from the people, even to the extent of having a separate elite dialect. The Spanish easily stripped the top layer of power away and took its place.

Pizarro was assassinated in 1541, only nine years after the capture of Atahualpa. He was for a time replaced by Diego de Almagro, the son of his fellow conqueror, also named Diego de Almagro. For the next seven years civil war raged among factions of the conquistadors. Worried by this, Spain sent a viceroy, Blasco Nuñez de Vela, in 1544. He was assassinated less than two years later. Spanish government forces were sent and quickly established control in 1548.

Disease proved to be more effective than warfare in conquering the native population. The indigenous people had no immunity to the various diseases the Europeans unwittingly brought with them, and quickly succumbed in astonishingly high numbers. The Spanish kept no records but did record observations that the native people were so devastated by disease that they often could barely resist conquest. The main culprit was smallpox, along with bubonic plague, influenza, and measles.

The Spanish conquest of the Inca had the effect, if not the intention, of genocide. From an estimated Peruvian Inca population of nine to twelve million in the 1520s, only about six hundred thousand remained by 1620. Infectious disease was the overwhelming cause of this extraordinarily rapid loss of people and their civilization.

COLONIAL PERU

The Spanish established a system called the *encomienda* (en-koh-MYEN-dah), whereby allotments of land and natives were given to their men to induce them to stay. This rapidly resulted in serfdom for the native population. Illness caused such a rapid decline in the local population, however, that it resulted in a labor shortage. The Spanish remedied this problem by importing slaves from Africa; by 1554, more than 1,500 enslaved people had arrived in Lima.

As Spain required more control in Peru than the independent *encomenderos* could provide, the Spanish government divided the country into *corregimientos* (kor-REJ-ee-mee-EN-tos),or units of land, each governed by a royal administrator who limited the power of the encomenderos, causing much friction between them.

In 1569 Francisco de Toledo was appointed Peru's fifth viceroy. He reformed the colonial system to increase revenue and also to improve the lot of the natives, who were increasingly being exploited as slaves. One of the ways de Toledo improved native life was by resettling people from remote places, where they were easily manipulated by the encomenderos, to cities and towns. Most of his reforms stood for many years but as time went on, became subject to abuses and exploitation.

The eighteenth century saw the start of uprisings. In Spain the Hapsburgs were replaced by the Bourbons, who tried to stem corruption in the colonies. This led to rebellion between supporters and opponents of the colonialist system in Peru. With the wave of revolutions over Europe and the Americas in the late eighteenth century, liberal ideas spread and a sense of national identity arose. The newspaper *Mercurio Peruano*, first printed in 1790, began to express concepts of Peruvian nationalism.

REBELLION AND REPUBLIC

When the French emperor Napoleon Bonaparte took control of Spain in 1808, the Spanish colonies were in a state of paralysis. Conflict between those loyal to the deposed Spanish king, Ferdinand VII, and those loyal to the followers of Joseph Bonaparte (Napoleon's brother, whom Napoleon had made king of Spain and Naples), became a source of agitation for revolution. Peru remained more attached to Spain than its Andean neighbors did, and it was only with the arrival of outside forces that Peruvian independence became a reality.

Venezuela and Argentina had already declared their independence, and General José de San Martín, one of the great liberators of South America, had in 1817 freed Chile from Spanish rule. San Martín decided it was necessary to liberate Peru, and in 1820 he landed on Peru's southern coast with five thousand men. On July 28, 1821, San Martín entered Lima and declared all of Peru a republic.

San Martín devised a constitution that gave freedom to the slaves, abolished native servitude, proclaimed the descendants of the Incas to be citizens of Peru, and even banned the insulting term *Indio*. This liberal constitution frightened many of his supporters into a more conservative frame of mind. San Martín returned home to Chile in 1822, leaving his army in Lima. He sought the help of Simón Bolívar, who had already liberated Venezuela, Colombia, and Ecuador, to decisively defeat the royalist armies, offering Bolívar the presidency. Bolívar was president of Peru between 1824 and 1826, and royalist troops were finally defeated at the Battle of Ayacucho

in 1824. San Martín's promises to abolish native servitude and to recognize Quechua as an official language were never kept.

In this painting, General José de San Martín proclaims Peru's independence in 1821.

A TROUBLED BEGINNING

For two decades there were many internal disputes between the aristocracy and the army. It was only with the presidency of General Ramón Castilla in 1845 that real stability was achieved. Under Castilla, Peru began to seriously exploit its vast and profitable deposits of guano, bird dung used as fertilizer that was found on remote islands. The Castilla administration organized public schools, abolished slavery, and began a railway network to interconnect most of Peru, especially the highlands.

Under Castilla's successors, Peru became increasingly debt-ridden, and its major export, guano, was exhausted. In 1879 Peru went to war with

Chile over valuable nitrate deposits in Peru and Bolivia. The four-year War of the Pacific ended with Peru's loss of the nitrate fields to Chile. Peru also lost ownership of much of its infrastructure and natural resources to foreigners.

In the forty years after independence from Spain, the presidency changed hands thirty-five times, and the country generated at least fifteen different constitutions. In this period only four of the presidents were constitutionally chosen, and the vast majority were military figures.

TWENTIETH CENTURY

Peru entered the twentieth century with some stability but was governed by rich businessmen and landowners. With the presidency of Augusto Leguía y Salcedo (1908—1912 and 1919—1930), the country rapidly expanded its mineral and agricultural industries and developed its oil reserves. Lima was modernized with beautiful plazas and parks, but the rest of the country remained unchanged.

Fernando Belaúnde Terry served as president of Peru from 1963 to 1968 and again from 1980 to 1985.

In 1963, Peru returned to civilian rule with Fernando Belaúnde Terry as president. The armed forces overthrew Belaúnde in the coup of 1968. They expanded the role of the state, nationalized several industries and embarked on agrarian reform. Plantations were turned into peasant cooperatives, while foreign companies and banks were nationalized. These initiatives failed miserably, and the economy remained problematic in the years ahead.

After twelve years of military rule, free elections were held and Belaúnde was reelected president in 1980. The Communist Party of Peru then emerged as Sendero Luminoso (sen-DER-oh loo-mee-NOH-soh) or "Shining Path," a Maoist guerrilla insurgent organization. (Maoist means based on the ideology of Chinese political leader Mao Zedong, 1893—1976.) Seeking to incite a communist revolution, the group staged ongoing armed conflict in Peru that resulted in 69,280 deaths from 1980 to 2000.

Another leftist militant group, the Tupac Amaru Revolutionary Movement (MRTA) followed a Marxist ideology. Although it, too, committed terrorist

THE SHINING PATH AND THE "PEOPLE'S WAR"

Inspired by China's Cultural Revolution in during the 1960s, the Communist Party of Peru launched an assault against the Peruvian government in 1980. Calling itself Sendero Luminoso or "Shining Path," the armed insurgent group began by aiming most of its attacks against peasants in the countryside. It then focused its attacks against the police and targeted civilians it deemed to be "class enemies." The government responded by sending the military into certain provinces where Shining Path infiltration was high.

The combat was particularly bloody and gruesome. Both the guerillas and the military forces committed scores of human rights violations, including numerous massacres of innocent civilians, many of them young children and pregnant women. The indigenous people formed patrols called rondas *to fight the Shining Path with guns donated by the military. Thus, a third contingent of Peruvians became involved in the violence that came to be called Peru's "internal conflict."*

In 1992, the Shining Path took its revolt to the cities and initiated a bombing campaign in Lima which resulted in forty deaths and tremendous damage to the city. Peruvian President Alberto Fujimori intensified his crackdown on domestic insurgent groups and suspended the country's constitution. His anti-communist death squads conducted massacres and human rights abuses as well.

The Shining Path suffered its biggest blow with the arrest of its founder, Abimael Guzmán in 1992 (shown at right). He was later sentenced to life in prison. In 1994, some six thousand Shining Path guerillas surrendered to the authorities. What was left of the weakened insurgency broke into smaller groups, which became more involved in drug trafficking. The main faction was led by Florindo Eleuterio Flores, alias Comrade Artemio, who was arrested in February 2012. At that time, Peruvian President Ollanta Humala declared the army's mission against the Shining Path accomplished. However, in August 2015, Peru's counterterror chief Jose Baella said the left-wing rebels still had some 350 members, and about eighty fighters.

In all, nearly seventy thousand people died or disappeared in more than a decade of internal conflict.

President Alberto Fujimori's removal in 2000 paved the way for Peru's reconciliation process. In 2001 the government set up the Truth and Reconciliation Commission (CVR) to investigate the political killings that devastated Peru from 1980 to 2000. During this period the civil war waged by Shining Path guerrillas and the Túpac Amaru Revolutionary Movement (MRTA) in Peru's remote regions completely wiped out certain indigenous communities.

After 17,000 testimonies, the commission released its final report in August 2003, concluding that 69,280 Peruvians had been killed or went missing in the violence on both sides. Over 11,500 cases of crimes against humanity were documented, including those of torture, massacre, rape, slavery, and kidnapping. The Shining Path was found to be responsible for 54 percent of the deaths, the Peruvian armed forces for 28 percent. The rest were attributed to civilian defense groups and the MRTA.

The majority of the victims belonged to the most marginalized groups, namely Quechua-speaking indigenous people, peasants, farmers, and rural dwellers. Some 600,000 inhabitants were displaced from their homes. Ethnic discrimination was one of the reasons why the suffering and fatalities of these defenseless civilians had gone unnoticed for twenty years.

Handing in the report, the chairman of the committee, Salomón Lerner said, "The report we hand in contains a double outrage: that of massive murder, disappearance and torture; and that of indolence, incompetence and indifference of those who could have stopped this humanitarian catastrophe but didn't."

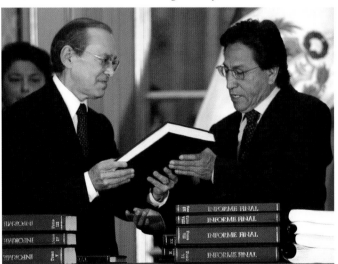

Peruvian philosopher Salomón Lerner (*left*) head of Peru's Truth and Reconciliation Commission, hands the completed report to President Alejandro Toledo in 2003.

Some 378 former military and police officers have been charged for gross human rights violations. The government has offered 2,845 million soles ($845 million) in compensation to the victims and their families. It will provide education grants to war orphans and funding for violence-affected areas. In May 2004, a new law recognized the special rights and needs of the displaced, including their eligibility for compensation.

The CVR set up a photographic archive and an exhibit called "Yuyanapaq," which means "To Remember" in Quechua. The exposition, which is displayed at Museum of the Nation

A man writes the name of his father at a symbolic graveyard of stones representing the victims of Peru's terrorist past.

in Lima, includes images of terrorist attacks, propaganda, torture victims, and other documentation of the horrors. The exhibition is open to the public.

acts, it never had the strength of numbers that Shining Path had, and was guilty of far fewer atrocities. It is best remembered for holding seventy-two people hostage at the Japanese ambassador's residence in Lima for more than four months in 1997. In the end, all fourteen of the MRTA militants involved in that event were killed.

In 1985 Alan García Pérez from the APRA (Alianza Popular Revolucionaria Americana) won the elections, but with the rise of terrorism, there seemed to be no resolution to Peru's divisions.

Peruvian President
Alberto Fujimori and
his daughter, Keiko,
wave to journalists
and supporters
after climbing to
the top of a gate
surrounding the
Presidential Palace
in Lima in
September 2000.

THE RISE AND FALL OF ALBERTO FUJIMORI

In 1990, political novice Alberto Fujimori, a Peruvian-born son of Japanese immigrants, defeated noted novelist Mario Vargas Llosa for the presidency. Fujimori's radical economic reforms included the privatization of state-owned companies. Fujimori staged a military coup in April 1992, suspended Congress, and declared a state of emergency to combat terrorism. September's capture of Shining Path's leader, Abimael Guzmán, diminished the rebels' grip on Peru.

Accusations of a tainted reelection and serious rioting eventually forced the disgraced president to resign in November 2000. He fled to Japan, and was shielded from extradition by Japanese citizenship, which was granted after his arrival. In November 2005, Fujimori was arrested in Chile while en route to Peru to take part in the April 2006 presidential elections.

In 2009, Peru's Supreme Court found Fujimori guilty of ordering two massacres in 1991 and 1992 during the government's battle against leftist guerrillas, and of involvement in other human rights abuses. Specifically, he was found guilty of murder, bodily harm, and two cases of kidnapping. The court sentenced him to twenty-five years in prison. Fujimori's conviction marked the first time in history that a democratically-elected president had been tried and found guilty of human rights abuses in his own country.

In 2011, Ollanta Humala (b. 1962), of the *Gana Perú* ("Peru Wins") party, won the presidency over Keiko Fujimori (b. 1975) of the *Fuerza 2011* ("Force 2011") party and daughter of the disgraced former president. Humala won in the run-off by 51.45 percent to Fujimori's 48.55 percent.

Fujimori ran again in 2016, winning nearly 6 million votes in the first round. The runner-up was Pedro Pablo Kuczynski, who received 3 million votes. The winner will be selected in a second round.

INTERNET LINKS

news.bbc.co.uk/2/hi/americas/country_profiles/1224690.stm
The BBC's Timeline: Peru lists events from 1532 to 2012.

www.cfr.org/peru/shining-path-tupac-amaru-peru-leftists/p9276
The US Council on Foreign Relations traces the history of the Peruvian leftist insurgencies.

www.cverdad.org.pe/ingles/pagina01.php
This is the site of the Truth and Reconciliation Committee.

www.discover-peru.org/category/history
This site has a wide range of articles relating to different aspects of Peru's history.

whc.unesco.org/en/list/274
The UNESCO World Heritage List page for Machu Picchu includes photos, maps, and links.

GOVERNMENT

The Peruvian Coat of Arms features a vicuña, a cinchona tree, and a cornucopia of coins—representing the nation's animals, plants, and mineral resources.

3

P ERU IS A CONSTITUTIONAL REPUBLIC
with independent executive,
legislative, and judicial branches of
government and a multiparty system. The
capital is Lima, on the country's Pacific
Coast, and one of South America's largest
cities. The Government Palace, which is
also called the House of Pizarro, is located
in Lima's historic center and serves as
both the seat of the executive branch of
the national government as well as the
presidential residence.

• • • • • • • • • • • •

The *vicuña*, a wild
South American
camelid which is
similar to a llama, is
the national symbol
of Peru. It is pictured
in the official coat of
arms, which appears
in the center of
the red and white
national flag.

THE CONSTITUTION

Peru's current constitution, approved by referendum on October 31, 1993,
is Peru's fifth in the twentieth century. The constitution was amended
in 2000 to prohibit the president from seeking reelection for a second
consecutive five-year term. This means Ollanta Humala, president since
2011, will end his term in 2016. The constitution was amended again in
2009 to address the legislative branch by adding that only Peruvians by
birth may run for Congress.

Voting is mandatory for citizens eighteen to seventy years of age,
except for those in the military and National Police. A candidate must

gain 50 percent of the vote to be directly elected as president. If none of the candidates can garner half the votes, a second round of voting will be conducted between the two strongest contenders. Prior to the 1979 constitution, there was a literacy requirement for voting, but that was eliminated.

THE EXECUTIVE

The president is the chief of state, head of government, and supreme chief of the armed forces and National Police. He or she oversees national defense and has the power to enforce laws, declare war and sign peace treaties, and order emergency decrees, among other responsibilities.

The first and second vice presidents are elected for the same term but have no constitutional functions unless the president cannot carry out his duties. Headed by the prime minister, the fifteen-member Council of Ministers (cabinet) approves legislative decrees and bills sent to Congress.

The president may not run for consecutive terms, but can run again after another president's term. The change of government takes place on July 28, Peru's Independence Day.

The Government Palace in Lima, also known as the House of Pizarro, dates to 1535.

THE LEGISLATURE

The legislative branch is a unicameral, or one-house, Congress, with 130 members elected at the same time as the president, also for five-year terms. Besides passing laws and amending or repealing existing laws, Congress is responsible for approving the budget, loans, and international treaties. The president can reject legislation that the executive branch does not approve. Congress can also appoint commissions to conduct investigations of public interest.

Over time, reforms have significantly improved decentralization and strengthened institutional checks and balances. In 2000, Congress dissolved the National Intelligence Service, abolished the state of emergency, and reinstated constitutional guarantees. In 2001, it recognized the jurisdiction of the Inter-American Court of Human Rights, and a 1995 amnesty that favored the military was lifted.

The tenure of legislative office is fixed at five years, and candidates for the presidency cannot become candidates for Congress

Peruvian President Ollanta Humala delivers a message to the nation in the Congress building in 2012.

THE JUDICIARY

The 1993 constitution provides for a Supreme Court of Justice, superior courts, specialized and mixed courts, justices of the peace, and lawyers. There is one Supreme Court for the entire country, while there is a Superior Court in each judicial district. Judges (except for justices of the peace, who are elected) are appointed and removed by the National Justice Council.

The Palace of Justice is a twentieth-century neoclassical style building located in Lima's city center.

The sixteen-member Supreme Court in Lima is the highest court in the land. Superior courts sit in regional capitals and hear appeals from lower courts. Courts in the provincial capitals are divided into civil, penal, and special chambers, and have jurisdiction over all serious crime. Justices of the peace are the lowest courts and have jurisdiction over petty crime and minor civil matters. These courts are found in most local towns.

The National Elections Board establishes voting laws, registers parties and their candidates, and supervises elections, which it has the power to void if there are irregularities. In 1996 the Office of the Human Rights Ombudsman was formed to protect the people's constitutional rights and to supervise the duties of the State and its public services.

REGIONAL AND LOCAL GOVERNMENT

The administration of Peru has traditionally been very centralized, and only recently have regional governments been given powers independent of the national government in Lima. Peru is divided into twenty-five administrative regions, including the constitutional province of Callao. All regions are further divided into provinces and subdivided into districts. There are 180 provinces and 1,747 districts. The city of Lima and greater Lima, however, do not belong to any particular region, and are referred to as Lima Metropolitana (Metropolitan Lima).

Since 2002, Peruvians have elected their own regional presidents and other local authorities. Under the Decentralization Framework Act, all decision-making powers, budget, and taxation authority were transferred to the twenty-five regional governments over a ten-year period. The regional governments manage their own infrastructure, revenues, and services, among other responsibilities. This move was meant to devolve power to provincial governments and improve public access to services.

The Municipal Palace in Lima was built in the twentieth century after the original building was destroyed by earthquake and fires.

INTERNET LINKS

www.cia.gov/library/publications/the-world-factbook/geos/pe.html
The CIA *World Factbook* keeps up to date information about Peru's government.

www.constituteproject.org/constitution/Peru_2009.pdf
The text of Peru's constitution is available in English on this pdf.

limaeasy.com/peru-info/peruvian-politics-political-history#humala
This site presents an overview of Peru's political history, the government structure, and the major political parties, with photos.

ECONOMY

Tourists look in awe at the rugged landscape of Arequipa.
Tourism is an important sector of Peru's economy.

4

ECONOMICALLY, THE NEWS OUT OF Peru in recent years has been good. in 2015, the World Bank said Peru's economy was one of the best performing economies in Latin America, where it is the seventh largest economy. From 2005 to 2014, the Peruvian economy grew by an average of 6.1 percent—well above the regional average—with a stable exchange rate and low inflation. Today, less than 30 percent of Peruvians live below the poverty line, down from about 60 percent a decade ago. Likewise, the population living below the extreme poverty line also declined dramatically, from 15.8 percent in 2005 to 4.3 percent in 2014.

Peru's economy reflects it geographical conditions, which support a variety of natural resources. The country's different climate zones allow for agricultural diversity, and its coastal waters provide excellent fishing grounds. The mountains and coastal areas have rich deposits of important minerals—Peru is the world's second largest producer of silver and third largest producer of copper.

MINING

The mining and hydrocarbon industries in the Andean and Amazonian regions produce about two-thirds of the country's exports. Foreign investment in these sectors is critical to the country's economic stability. Between 2000 and 2012, investment in Peruvian mining rose from around $300 million to $8.6 billion—a huge increase—and accounted for nearly 50 percent of all private investment projects in the country.

The La Oroyo mineral refinery has caused such tremendous pollution that the surrounding city has been called one of the ten most polluted places on Earth.

Mining contributes nearly 15 percent of Peru's gross domestic product, generates 10 to 16 percent of the country's tax revenues, and provides more than two hundred thousand jobs per year. China is the top investor in Peru's mining industry, investing some $19.2 billion into different copper mining projects. US-based companies are the next biggest investors, with $10.13 billion, followed by Canadian firms with $8.35 billion.

OIL AND GAS

Peru began exporting oil in the late nineteenth century when oil fields were first developed on the north coast. New fields were discovered in the Amazon region, and when the petroleum industry was nationalized in 1968 as Petroperu (privatized in 1993), these new fields began to be developed. A billion-dollar pipeline was completed in 1976 to pipe oil from the jungle over the Andes to the coast. Today, Peru has six oil refineries. Exploration of oil fields in Peru's Amazon rainforest is limited because of social conflicts and environmental considerations.

Crude oil production began to decline in the 1990s, falling from a high of 195,000 barrels a day in 1980 to 63,000 in 2013. However, this has been offset by an increased production of natural gas to satisfy its energy needs.

MINING OPPOSITION AND VIOLENCE

In 2016, some forty-seven new mining ventures were set to begin in Peru. The largest of the Chinese-backed projects, the Las Bambas copper, zinc, silver and gold mine, was scheduled to begin production. However, anti-mining sentiment is powerful in Peru. Protests in recent years have left a number of people dead and dozens injured, and have stalled some $21.5 billion worth of mining projects, including the Tia Maria copper mine in the Arequipa region of Peru.

The proposed Tia Maria mine would tap into one of the largest copper reserves in the world. The site holds an estimated 707 million tons (641 million metric tons) of ore. Southern Copper Corporation of Mexico, which wants to invest $1.4 billion into the mine, has been confronted with local protests since 2009, when it first proposed the project. In the spring of 2015, another four people died in mine-related violence. Peruvian President Ollanta Humala declared a state of emergency and called in the military. Thousands of police and soldiers were sent in and constitutional rights were suspended. More fighting ensued and more than two hundred people were injured—all of which only caused more protests.

The indigenous farmers of the region say the project's open pits will ruin their land in the Tambo Valley, dry up a good part of their water, and contaminate the rest. The protesters point to the mining company's past environmental record and find plenty of evidence to back up their claims. The government, for its part, is trying to improve the country's economic situation by bringing in more international investment.

Another problem facing the industry is illegal mining. Puerto Madonado, the capital of the Madre de Dios region of Peru is one of the world's most biodiverse places. It's also where some 70 percent of Peru's illicit gold mining takes place. About thirty thousand illegal gold miners are thought to labor there, clearing vast swaths of rain forest. Gold mining is a particularly toxic process, and without environmental safeguards in place, the illegal mining is turning forests into toxic wastelands. Some experts suspect that illegal gold mining brings more illicit money into the country than drug trafficking.

Oil from a pipeline leak seeps to the surface in the town of Nuevo Andoas in 2013.

In 2004 the Camisea natural gas project began its operations. Composed of several natural gas fields located in the Urubamba Valley of the Peruvian Amazon, Camisea fuels an electricity generator and six industrial plants in Lima. The gas there is equivalent to 2.4 million barrels of oil, about seven times the size of Peru's oil reserves. Pipelines carry the gas from the Amazon to Peru's coastal cities. It provides for domestic consumption and is expected to transform Peru into a net energy exporter.

The project is not without controversy, however, as there have been multiple spillages along the pipeline over the years. The gas project's effect on isolated indigenous people and animal life in the Amazon is also a concern which has prompted the UN to call for the 'immediate suspension' of any plans to expand Camisea.

AGRICULTURE

In the last two decades, Peru has emerged as a major exporter of fruits and vegetables. Asparagus, in particular, has been an enormously successful crop. For the most part, the boom has been good news for Peru's economy, but conflicts have arisen as large agribusinesses compete with small subsistence farmers for land and limited water resources.

The agricultural sector accounts for 7 percent of Peru's GDP and employs about 26 percent of the labor force. Climatic conditions in the countryside make possible the cultivation of different crops throughout the year, including sugarcane, potato, rice, corn, tomato, and jojoba, which yields a valuable wax used in cosmetics. It provides half the world's supply of quinoa. It also has a wide variety of fruit and medicinal plants such as cat's claw and maca. Almost 80 percent of agricultural workers own small plots of land or are peasants who communally share pasture. Most farmers produce mainly for themselves.

Before 1968, most land was divided into large estates that were owned by a small minority. The 1969 agrarian reform transformed the estates

COCA: WHITE GOLD

To the Incas, coca was known as the divine plant. Because coca was used in religious festivals and rites to induce ecstasies and visions, it was regarded as a sacred plant. Coca continued to be accepted after the conquest—even the Spanish clergy were enthusiastic about it. Chewing coca leaves suppresses hunger, thirst, and exhaustion, allowing people to do more work than normal, supposedly double their ordinary workload. The Spanish conquistadors found it vital in manipulating the natives, who were given large quantities of the leaves and literally worked to death in the silver and gold mines. Before the Spanish conquest, coca leaves were used only occasionally, to stave off hunger caused by a shortage of food or to lighten the burden of work, and this continues today.

In the nineteenth century coca and its more potent derivative, cocaine, were thought to be good for health, especially when made into a tonic or wine. This quickly changed as cocaine became recognized as a powerful, addictive, and deadly drug. In Peru cocaine is illegal, but coca leaves are not.

Past attempts to decrease or destroy the cocaine trade were usually met with failure. Buying up the crop or substituting different crops were almost impossible strategies because of the rapid increase in land devoted to coca growing. No other crop is anywhere near as profitable as coca. Coca is three times more profitable than cocoa and almost forty times more than corn.

Peasants will only abandon coca cultivation if legitimate means to earn a stable livelihood are available. The United Nations Office on Drugs and Crime (UNODC) has stepped up its alternative livelihood programs across the Andean region. UNODC data indicate that farmers involved in its program, such as those in palm oil production, earn three times more than their counterparts who are involved in coca cultivation.

In 2015, UNODC reported that the area of land used to grow coca in Peru had declined to its smallest level in fifteen years. In 2014, the report said, 106,000 acres (42,900 ha) of land were used for coca production, down 14 percent from the prior year.

into peasant cooperatives. About 24 million acres (10 million ha) of agricultural land were expropriated, and four hundred thousand families benefited. In the 1980s, the land was divided into small plots, placing more stress on individual enterprise. Overall, this policy was not successful, because the land usually provided insufficient yields to sustain small farms. Moreover, the farmers often lacked enough capital to sell their produce.

Crowds of sun worshippers enjoy a beach in the Chorrillos district of Lima.

TOURISM

Peru is an attractive South American destination for tourists. Peruvians are hospitable, and the country offers much to the tourist in terms of natural beauty, historical sites, and cultural variety. During the 1990s, the tourism industry suffered because of crime, attacks on tourists, and the terrorist threat. However, as the economy and political situation stabilized in the twenty-first century, tourism soared, becoming Peru's third largest industry, behind fishing and mining. It is also Peru's fastest growing industry; in fact, tourism is growing faster there than in any other South American country.

In 2011, nearly 2.6 million international tourists visited Peru. The travel and tourism sector made up about 3.4 percent of the country's gross domestic product (GDP)—GDP is an economic measure of a country's productivity—and provided jobs for more than three hundred thousand people.

Top attractions include Machu Picchu and other ancient Incan sites. The Cuzco Region is the most visited in Peru—the city of Cuzco, the former capital of the Incan Empire, is on the list of UNESCO's World Heritage sites. Lima and the other major cities, with their Spanish colonial architecture, restaurants, and museums of art, anthropology, archaeology, and history, are also popular cultural destinations. Ecotourism is important in the Amazon rain forests while adventure and sports tourism brings people to the mountains and the coast.

INTERNET LINKS

america.aljazeera.com/multimedia/2015/9/Peru-mining.html
The article, "Grim Prospects for sustainable miners in Peru" examines illegal gold mining.

www.desertsun.com/story/news/environment/2015/12/10/costs-perus-farming-boom/76605530
This in-depth story of a conflict between large agribusiness and local farmers over water in Peru.

www.focus-economics.com/countries/peru
This site offers a good basic overview and assessment of Peru's economy.

www.peru.travel/en-us
This site is Peru's official travel and tourism portal.

www.pri.org/stories/2012-01-23/despite-economic-gains-perus-asparagus-boom-threatening-water-table
Here, find a good explanation and infographic about how asparagus is causing water problems in Peru.

proof.nationalgeographic.com/2014/04/28/finding-the-faces-of-farming-a-peruvian-potato-harvest
This is a beautiful photo essay about Peruvian potato farmers.

ENVIRONMENT

The Llanganuco Lakes, Chinancocha and Orconcocha, are part of Huascarán National Park in the Cordillera Blanca.

5

B Y ANY MEASURE, PERU IS AN environmental treasure. It is one of the ten most biodiverse countries on Earth, blessed with an astonishing array of ecosystems, plant species, and wildlife. Its mosaic of landscapes—coastal deserts, Andean highlands, and Amazonian forests—are host to more than 80 percent of Earth's ecological zones.

Peru is the largest producer and exporter of the camu camu fruit (*Myrciaria dubia*), which grows in the Amazon rainforest. It has the highest vitamin C concentration of any food, about sixty times that of an orange, and is being touted as the next big health food.

Camu camu fruit grows on small bushy trees along rivers in the Amazon.

Signs of deforestation in Peru

Human activities, however, endanger Peru's natural treasure. The country's resources have long been overexploited, thanks in large part to government inaction. Peru has some five thousand laws and regulations pertaining to environmental protection and resource conservation. However, most of these are not enforced or are only partially implemented. Some of the problems lie with the institutional weakness of environmental agencies (limited political power, scant human and economic resources); unregulated industries that continue to degrade the environment; weak deterrence and punishment mechanisms; and the lack of a long-term national development strategy for the environment.

Deforestation, uncontrolled logging, pollution, dumping of mining wastes, overfishing, overgrazing, desertification, and extensive coca cultivation are just some of Peru's major environmental concerns.

DEFORESTATION

Peru is one of the most forested countries in the world. According to the United Nations Food and Agriculture Organization (FAO), more than 169 million acres (68 million hectares) or 53.7 percent, of Peru's territory is covered in natural-growth forest. This ranks Peru as the country with the fourth-largest tropical forest area. In the Peruvian Amazon, the main culprits of deforestation are small-scale agriculture, commercial mining and related road construction. Forest degradation is caused primarily by illegal logging, which makes up about 80 percent of all logging activity in Peru.

About 70 percent of Peru's forests are in the Amazon Basin—one of the oldest, largest, richest, and most complex ecosystems on Earth. Located in the country's eastern regions, the rain forest provides a habitat for an immense range of organisms and acts as a watershed for the planet's aquatic systems. More importantly, it serves as a regulator of the earth's climate.

Unfortunately, much of the Amazon Basin is under threat. The FAO estimates that the country loses somewhere between 554,000 and 741,000 acres (224,000 and 300,000 ha) of forest per year. This is largely attributed to agricultural, logging, and farming activities. Using the slash-and-burn technique, dense forests are cleared for cattle grazing and crop cultivation, while roads are built for logging. Overgrazing by livestock loosens the soil and leads to soil erosion. Even the mighty cloud forests in the Andes have been deforested by unsustainable potato farming and dairy production.

A deforested plot can be burned just twice before it becomes infertile. Studies have shown that leaving the rain forests intact, with their wealth of latex, nuts, and medicinal plants, has far greater economic value than destroying them for unsustainable short-term interests. When these natural habitats are destroyed, indigenous people lose their land, livelihood, and culture, and plant and animal species become extinct.

Another leading cause of deforestation is Peru's most controversial export—coca. Severe poverty drives peasant farmers to cultivate coca for

Plumes of smoke reveal slash-and-burn land clearing being carried out by migrant farmers.

the production of cocaine. Large areas on the Andean hillsides are destroyed for illegal plantations, which supply about two-thirds of the world's cocaine. As coca crops tend to rob the land of nutrients and cause soil erosion, replacement crops cannot be grown.

In addition, farmers spray pesticides on the plants, contaminating the soil and nearby waterways. Toxic chemicals are also widely used by local authorities to eradicate the illegal crop.

LOGGING

Throughout the Amazon Basin, commercial loggers, illegal and legal, are plundering the forests in search of prized timber such as mahogany and cedar. According to the Research Institute of the Peruvian Amazon, as much as 95 percent of the endangered mahogany from Peru is logged illegally. Mahogany is called "red gold" because a single tree can be worth tens of thousands of dollars in the international market. Its high value attracts prospectors who bulldoze deep into the forests and even into national parks and nature reserves.

Logging is also impacting indigenous people who depend on the forest for survival. Edwin Chota, an Asháninka native, worked for years as a well-known and outspoken advocate for indigenous rights. The main focus of his work was putting an end to the illegal logging industry that is destroying his

Logs from the Amazon jungle are carried on the river to the nearest harbor.

people's ancestral homelands. In September 2014, Chota and three other members of his community were killed by a group of illegal loggers.

Chota's murder made international headlines and drew further attention to the charge that the Peruvian government does nothing to stop the illegal loggers who terrorize the indigenous communities.

AIR, WATER, AND LAND POLLUTION

Some 60 percent of all solid waste in Lima is thrown into makeshift dumps, nearby rivers and oceans, or used in illegal livestock operations. A startling 40 percent of the entire population does not have access to waste disposal facilities; hence, waste is often dumped or burned. Industrial and household wastes, including those from fish meal production, contaminate the coastal rivers and lakes, while waterways in the Amazon Basin are sterile due to sludge deposits from oil extractions.

Mines dump cyanide, mining waste, and mercury into the streams, while smelter emissions pollute the air, especially in the highlands. Almost

In Belen, Iquitos, houses stand on stilts above the polluted water of the Itaya River, a tributary of the Amazon. The people live in extreme poverty without clean water or sanitation.

15 million gallons (57 million L) of liquid waste from coca processing have been discarded into the waters and on land. Heavy metal has been found in virtually every sample of sediment that was analyzed along the coast, as well as in marine life.

ENDANGERED SPECIES

The spectacled bear, giant river otter, marine turtle, mountain tapir, jaguar, and Humboldt penguin are among the one hundred or so Peruvian wildlife species that are threatened or endangered. The yellow-tailed woolly monkey, for example, is a very rare species found only in the Peruvian Andes. In 2010, it was considered critically endangered and one of the world's twenty-five most endangered primates. The Andean condor and the Andean mountain cat are other endangered mountain species in Peru.

The spectacled bear lives in the Andes.

Illegal trade in wildlife is a multibillion-dollar business. Exotic animals are captured alive and sold as pets or for research. Some are killed for their body parts and sold as food, clothing, accessories, and medicine. Others, like primates and lizards, are raised in captivity for the international market. Wild plants are commonly traded for use in botanical and pharmaceutical products. For many of these endangered plants and animals, such trade can lead to their extinction and is, therefore, a great threat to the ecological system and global biodiversity.

In 2016, Peru made its first felony arrest for illegal species trafficking, in this case, the capture and transport of a single ocelot. The event set an important precedent because the government has been criticized for doing nothing to counteract the theft and marketing of its wild animals. Although there are no statistics, Peru is thought to have the highest level of illegal trade in live animals in Latin America, and yet has one of the lowest rates of government enforcement.

PROTECTED AREAS

Peru has set aside forty-nine natural areas, including eight national parks, for conservation. These cover about 10 percent of Peru's land, and include the Manú Biosphere Reserve, the Tambopata-Candamo Reserve Zone, and the Pacaya-Samiria National Reserve, which are three of the largest protected rain forest areas in the world. UNESCO has designated the Huascarán National Park (in Huaráz), Manú National Park (in Madre de Dios), and Río Abiseo National Park (in San Martín) as World Heritage Sites.

Home to the spectacled bear and the Andean condor, Huascarán National Park's deep ravines, glacial lakes, and the world's highest tropical mountain peak, Mount Huascarán, make it a site of spectacular beauty. The massive Manú National Park is equally impressive—the rare giant otter, giant armadillo, and jaguar seek refuge there. Rain forests with characteristics that are unique to the Andes are protected in the Río Abiseo National Park. The yellow-tailed woolly monkey is also endemic, or native, to the area.

Chakrarahu Mountain in the Huascarán National Park is one of Peru's most distinctive-looking peaks.

In 2015, Peruvian President Ollanta Humala approved the creation of a 3.3 million-acre (1.3 million ha) national park at Sierra del Divisor. The new park, which is larger than Yosemite and Yellowstone National Parks combined, protects a great expanse of Amazon rain forest. It secures the final link in the 67 million-acre (27 million ha) Andes-Amazon Conservation Corridor, a contiguous complex of protected areas in the Amazon considered vital to the protection of wildlife biodiversity and indigenous communities. The corridor extends for more than 1,100 miles (1,609 km) from the Amazon River in Brazil to the Peruvian Andes.

ECO GROUPS

An increasing number of environmental organizations and movements now exist in Peru to protect the environment and preserve the indigenous people's culture and rights. INRENA, the National Institute of Natural Resources, enforces logging regulations and reseeds Peru's share of the Amazon forest.

A handful of international and local conservation groups, such as ProNaturaleza, Conservation International, and the Rainforest Action Network are active, working on reforestation and sustainable forestry projects in Peru.

The Amazon Rescue Center in Iquitos, in the Peruvian Amazon, works to save wildlife, particularly the Amazonian manatee, from the illegal wildlife trade.

The ACEER Foundation (Amazon Center for Environmental Education and Research) is a unique research center that aims to improve local awareness of the environment. Located within a 24,711-acre (10,000 ha) reserve at Tambopata, it offers education and research programs for scientists and students.

INTERNET LINKS

www.coha.org/the-ashaninka-illegal-logging-threatening-indigenous-rights-and-sustainable-development-in-the-peruvian-amazon
This very compelling article includes information about the killing of activist Edwin Chota in 2014.

ngm.nationalgeographic.com/2013/04/mahogany/wallace-text
This is an in-depth feature story about the work of Edwin Chota and illegal logging in Peru.

theplate.nationalgeographic.com/2015/03/23/deforestation-threatens-perus-food-system-environment
This article offers a look at how just one fruit contributes to the deforestation problem in Peru.

www.rainforesttrust.org/news/sierra-del-divisor-created
A map of Peru's Sierra del Divisor National Park and the Andes-Amazon Conservation Corridor can be found on this site.

upperamazon.org
The Upper Amazon Conservancy works to protect the environment and people of the Peruvian rainforest.

www.worldwildlife.org/magazine/issues/fall-2015/articles/deforestation-in-peru
This in-depth article focuses on deforestation, with excellent imagery.

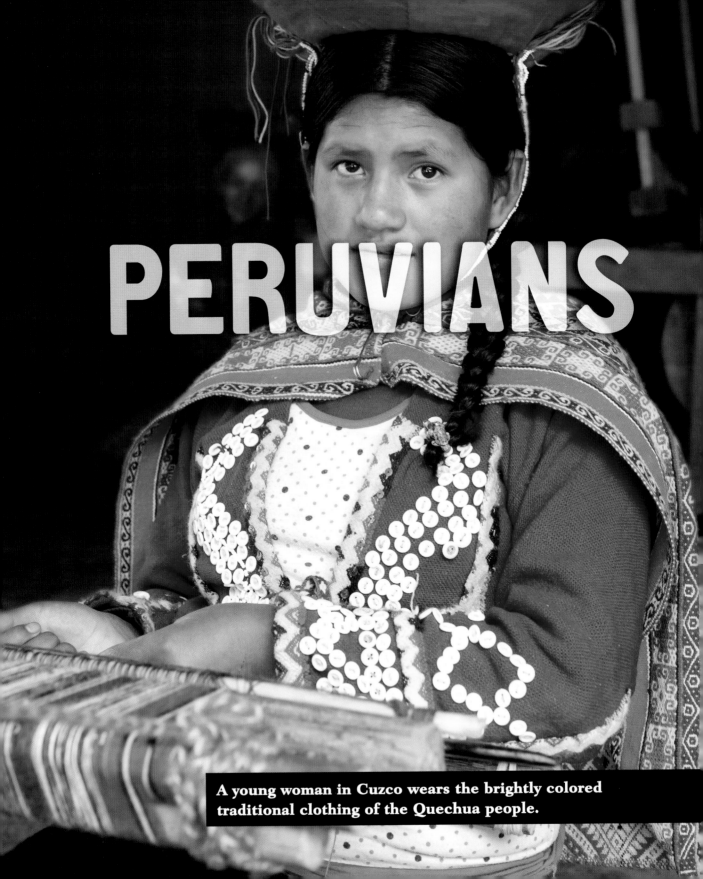

PERUVIANS

A young woman in Cuzco wears the brightly colored traditional clothing of the Quechua people.

PERU IS HOME TO ABOUT THIRTY million people, who represent a wide variety of ethnic groups. Intermarriage among the groups over the centuries has made racial classification difficult, because many distinctions are largely a matter of personal identity. People of mixed Spanish and native ancestry are *mestizo* (mes-TEE-zoh), but there are many variations and degrees of mixed heritage that are mostly culturally defined.

Officially, Peru's ethnic mix is: European, 15 percent; mestizos, 37 percent; indigenous, 45 percent; and African, Japanese, Chinese, and others, 3 percent. Other surveys find different numbers, depending on the labels offered for self-identification; but in any case, the mestizo and indigenous population makes up the largest portion of the population by far.

SOCIAL CLASSES

The Spanish conquerors established a class system based on race, one in which the white upper class ruled the lower class of native people. In the twentieth century, a middle class of mostly mestizos developed. Today most people remain in the social class they were born into; education is the main avenue for advancement.

The coastal and mountain regions have quite different elite, middle, and lower classes, the urbanization of the coast having produced totally different social conditions from the rural Sierra.

THE ELITE The coastal elite, numbering only a small percentage of the total population, is composed of people from various prestigious backgrounds: members of the agricultural aristocracy, successful immigrants or their children, and the Peruvian representatives of foreign businesses. Descendants from the old Spanish families form one of the largest segments of the elite.

The wealth of the elite class comes from banking, finance, marketing, land ownership, or industry. Until the military coup of 1968, forty-four families dominated Peruvian affairs in nearly every sphere. This small number owned a substantial amount of the land, estimated at more than 70 percent of the country.

The military dictatorship, which was mainly middle-class and mestizo, stripped these families of some of their wealth, but the redistribution still went mainly to the top 25 percent of the population. Most of the elite live in Lima and Callao, less often in Trujillo and Arequipa. Those who live in the Sierra have declined in significance as their power in local government and agriculture has been eroded. Estates were divided by inheritance laws and families became less influential until, in 1969, nearly all land holdings were taken from them.

One of the main ways the elite on the coast retained their privileges was to diversify into business and finance instead of relying on their private estates for wealth. They have also used kinship bonds to incorporate the newly rich into their society and strengthen ties with other families.

THE MIDDLE CLASS About 57 percent of Peruvians consider themselves to be middle class, a number that has risen significantly in recent years. Like the elite, the middle class is mainly urban, educated, and speaks Spanish. Peru's middle class looks to the elite for its values. It is not surprising that over half the middle class is employed by the government.

The middle class in the Sierra is wholly dependent on cheap native labor and is itself in the employ of the elite, looking after their estates and filling local government and administrative posts. With recent political events and the elites' diminishing power, the middle class is now taking the lead in the creation of a new and modern Peru.

THE LOWER CLASS The lower class is highly diverse, including nearly 80 percent of the population. It includes the unemployed, laborers, small farmers, small shopkeepers, itinerant traders, artisans, servants, and enlisted military personnel.

Because of this diversity, the lower class has great difficulty in forming an organized front or creating a union powerful enough to take on the bosses. Farm laborers have little in common with small farm owners. Even highly skilled union members find it more advantageous to make alliances with the middle-class professional unions.

The family is one of the most important aspects of life for the lower class. Marriages in the Sierra are more stable than those in the coastal areas. Parental authority is also more evident and respected in the Sierra.

Families gather and organize entertainment, fiestas, soccer games, and dances that the whole community enjoys. Associations springing from family ties and affiliations also try to organize political and economic activities, pressuring politicians and local landowners for support or change.

IMMIGRANTS

Before independence, Peru was not open to immigration, and the only foreign arrivals were the African slaves imported to work on plantations. Foreigners began arriving in Peru in the 1830s. Compared with Brazil or Argentina, immigration was not large scale and was usually work-related. Chinese immigrants came between 1850 and 1875 to work on the railroads and guano deposits.

Today, the number of Peruvians of Chinese descent is perhaps 1.3 million. Many Japanese arrived in Peru in the early twentieth century, and today around 160,000 people of Japanese descent live there. In the business

community, British and North Americans are the biggest groups, but there are also a small number of Europeans and Arabs. The neighboring countries of Colombia, Chile, Bolivia, and Ecuador have also contributed new residents.

NATIVE PEOPLES

The indigenous people can be subdivided into two groups, those from the Andes Sierra region and those from the Amazon jungles.

THE ANDEAN PEOPLE The Aymara and the Quechua populate central and southern Andes. The Quechua live mainly in the Sierra departments of Ancash, Ayacucho, and Cuzco. Several other departments, or administrative subdivisions, that have a high proportion of Quechua speakers are Junín, Huánuco, Huancavelica, and Apurímac. The Aymara are found mainly in Puno, although many have migrated to the southern departments of Arequipa, Moquegua, and Tacna. Because of steady migration in the twentieth century, substantial numbers of both native groups now live in the cities, especially Lima.

The Aymara and Quechua live side by side, although there is little intermarriage between them. The Aymara are likely to speak Spanish and Quechua; the Quechua, Spanish. They both hold stereotyped views of each other: the Aymara consider the Quechua old-fashioned, uneducated, and lazy, whereas the Quechua think the Aymara are stubborn, argumentative, and money-minded.

Some mestizos and whites look down on the indigenous people. The natives are widely despised by other Peruvians, who hold them to be inferior, drunken, superstitious, dirty, lazy, and addicted to coca. Despite reforms in the 1970s, the natives are still dislocated from the rest of the country's people. Some indigenous families who have risen socially go to great lengths to mask their origins.

A Quechua woman wears Western clothing in a mountain village above Ollantaytambo in southern Peru.

There is, however, a great deal of social mobility between the natives and mestizos. Natives who adopt Spanish as their main language, don Western rather than traditional clothing, and take up a mestizo occupation are called *cholos*, an insulting term that suggests the person is trying to rise above his or her proper social place.

THE AMAZON PEOPLE A much more diverse collection of tribes lives east of the Andes in the Amazon Basin. Although there are only around 350,000 natives in the Peruvian Amazon, they belong to sixty-five different ethnic groups and speak sixteen main languages and many varied dialects. Some tribes have only a handful of members still living, whereas others, like the Jívaro and the Asháninka, are doing very well.

The Amazonian peoples have a fierce and warlike reputation. The Incas, although powerful builders of an empire, could not subdue them, and there are many legends of hordes of Amazons repeatedly sacking Cuzco. Generally, the Incas left these people alone, except to trade with them in cloth, bronze, axes, exotic fruits, and wood. When the Spanish arrived, they, too, were confronted with various tribes who would not accept their authority. Expeditions into the jungle ended in Spanish annihilation.

One of the fiercest and most interesting Amazon tribes thriving today is the Jívaro, who have resisted all attempts to conquer them. They still live in their tropical forest homeland to the east of the Andes. The Jívaro fish and hunt with blowguns and poison darts. They keep domestic animals, gather berries and roots from the forest, and plant banana trees and manioc, a root vegetable. On small handlooms men weave cloth into kilt-like skirts, which are worn by both men and women. Chiefs and shamans wear feathers denoting their status. Each small white bone worn on the left shoulder of a warrior represents a man he has killed. Women usually wear robes pinned on one shoulder, but some people wear ponchos.

Children stand in the doorway of a thatched hut in a village on the Amazon River.

An Asháninka family eats a meal in their jungle home.

Family life revolves around the house, which can hold thirty to forty relatives. Polygamy is common because of the shortage of men due to warfare, mostly waged between different Jívaro communities.

The Asháninka, to the east of the Andes, are similar to the Jívaro in that they were never conquered by either the Incas or the Spanish. During the rubber boom (1839–1913), however, the Asháninka were enslaved by rubber tappers and about 80 percent of the population was killed. In addition to the rubber tappers, loggers, Shining Path guerrillas, drug traffickers, colonizers, missionary groups, and oil companies have encroached upon and destroyed the tribe's lands.

The Asháninka have much more contact with the outside world than the Jívaro, and this has influenced their culture. Occasionally a tribe can minimize the damage done to their culture by outside influences. For example, the Shipibo of central Peru, who live along the Ucayali River, have a cooperative selling their pottery and weavings to museums and shops from around the world.

Clothing is made from jungle materials—bark cloth is reddened with dye and worn like a robe. Men and boys hunt pigs, deer, and monkeys, and fish for food. Traditionally, agriculture is considered women's work. Women grow bananas, yucca, sugarcane, and coca.

In other regions of the Amazon rain forests, there remain isolated groups of people that are classified as "uncontacted tribes." One organization, Survival International, estimates there are fifteen such tribes in Peru. These people live in the same way they have for centuries. Most of these tribes have made it clear they do not want interference. First contact with the outside world is often followed by a large number of deaths among the tribespeople, mainly from disease. Sometimes, the entire tribe perishes. Today, these people face grave threats from illegal loggers, miners, and oil workers that are increasingly encroaching on their territories.

PERUVIAN ATTIRE

People who live in the cities and towns, as well as mestizos who live in rural areas, wear Western dress. Traditional dress is more frequently worn by indigenous people in the rural areas.

The Spanish changed every aspect of native life when they came to Peru. That included introducing new materials such as sheep's wool (the Incas used alpaca wool) and silk. Tailoring was also introduced. During the 1570s and 1580s and after the native revolts of the late eighteenth century, the Spanish issued edicts forbidding the wearing of traditional clothing, which they saw as a sign of native nationalism. By around 1700, a native man with high social status would wear European-style clothing, whereas the women persisted in wearing Inca-style dress.

NATIVE MEN'S DRESS   Contemporary native dress is a mixture of Western and Incan. Men's pants and shirts are European. The shirt, called *kutun* (KOO-tun), is made of wool or cotton and usually factory-made or made by local market tailors. The pants, or *pantalones* (pan-tah-LO-nes), are made from handwoven flannel-like wool cloth of one color, usually black, which is called *bayeta* (bay-YET-ah). A bayeta vest or waistcoat is sometimes worn over a shirt, called a *chaleco* (cha-LEH-koh). Sandals are made either of tire rubber or leather and, if not made in the home, can be found in most markets.

Each village has different patterns or colors associated with it that are reproduced on the costumes, and this applies to hats as well. Brimmed hats called *monteras* (mon-TEH-rahs) are very common. The style is reminiscent of Spanish colonial hats. A more traditional version is the *chullo* (CHOO-yoh), a handknit hat with ear flaps that is sometimes worn under the montera. It is usually brightly colored and can be decorated with buttons. Originally the chullo came from the Aymara people, but it can now be seen all over the highlands.

The warlike Shuar people, one of four Jívaroan subtribes, are the infamous headhunters of the Peruvian and Ecuadorian Amazon jungle. Their ferociousness—and especially their practice of shrinking heads—have historically aroused fear and fascination among Amazon explorers, missionaries, and anthropologists. Violence and killing are a vital part of the Jívaro culture. The more a man kills, the more powerful he himself becomes. In their view, sickness and death are not natural, but are the result of invisible attacks on their souls by malicious shamans. The stronger one's soul, the more it can resist and repel such attacks.

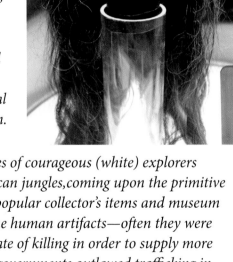

Traditionally, Shuar men collect the heads of the people they kill in tribal feuds. They believe the head contains the victim's soul, which will seek revenge for the murder. Shrinking the head prevents the avenging soul, or muisak, *from escaping and asserting its will.*

Making a shrunken head, or tsantsa, *is a ritualistic process. First, the skull and interior organs are removed and the eyes and lips sewn shut. A wooden ball is inserted to keep the shape, and the head is boiled in water containing tannic herbs until it shrinks to about one-third its size. Next, the head is dried and remolded into its human form. Charcoal ash and decorative accessories are applied to the skin.*

In the late nineteenth and early twentieth centuries, Western audiences were captivated by tales of courageous (white) explorers who ventured deep into the uncharted South American jungles,coming upon the primitive "savages" who lived there. Shrunken heads became popular collector's items and museum pieces. As customers began buying up these gruesome human artifacts—often they were traded for guns and knives—tribes increased their rate of killing in order to supply more heads. By the 1930s, the Peruvian and Ecuadorian governments outlawed trafficking in human heads, and the practice went into decline.

Today, some tribes produce fake tsantsas out of monkey or sloth heads for the tourist trade. In fact, some experts think up to 80 percent of the tsantsas in collections and museums may be counterfeit replicas. In general, the practice has died out among the Jívaro peoples, but it's possible that small splinter groups still continue the ritual.

NATIVE WOMEN'S DRESS Women wear their hair in two braids, which are then tied together at the back. Like the men, they wear a montera and sandals. The skirt, or *pollera* (po-YEH-rah), is a full-gathered wool skirt, usually with a decorated hem. Traditionally they are black, but they can be found in navy blue, pink, yellow, or orange. On festival days, a woman will wear as many pollera as possible to signify her wealth. Most women own only one or two. Around Cuzco, a short jacket, or *saco* (SAH-koh), which is ornamented with braids and buttons, is worn. The belt is the same as a man's.

Amanta, worn by nearly every woman as a shawl, is a rectangular or square piece of handwoven cloth. If a village has a particular color or design on its ponchos, it is usually repeated on the manta. To keep the manta in place, a *tupo* (TOO-poh), or small pin, is used. This has a flat, hammered, circular head with knife-sharp edges. The pins vary in design and can be in the shape of flowers or birds and trees. Depending on what class the woman belongs to, the pin will be made of copper, silver, or gold.

In 1999, the National Museum of the American Indian in Washington, DC, returned its entire collection of authentic shrunken heads to Ecuador.

INTERNET LINKS

www.discovernikkei.org/en/journal/2007/5/24/japanese-person-in-peru
This memoir relates how it was to grow up as a person of Japanese descent in Peru.

www.survivalinternational.org/tribes/isolatedperu
This site focuses on uncontacted tribes in Peru and includes videos.

upperamazon.org
The Upper Amazon Conservancy works to protect the isolated tribal people of the Peruvian jungle.

LIFESTYLE

A child works as a souvenir vendor in Colca Canyon, a popular tourist site.

7

PRESENT-DAY PERUVIANS LIVE IN a rapidly changing society. Recent economic upheavals, combined with intense urban migration and improvements in transportation and communications, have had a profound effect on the lives of many Peruvians.

Old ways are disappearing or being adapted to new influences. Changes in women's roles, the growth of the middle class, and public education are bringing new opportunities to the entire population.

An Andean family poses with their llama in Cuzco.

Peruvians who live in urban areas mostly wear western style clothes and have lifestyles that are similar to those of most Europeans or Americans. People who live in the highlands and rural areas, however, mostly wear traditional clothing-especially the women.

As a nation, Peruvians have long experience in adapting to changing influences. Under the domination of the Incas and later the Spanish, Peru's people have learned to resist oppression and renew themselves in adverse conditions. Like their ancestors, modern Peruvians are once again experiencing the process of resisting and renewing.

ROLES OF WOMEN AND MEN

Peru is generally a man's world, and the Hispanic concept of *machismo* (ma-CHEES-moh), which defines masculine attributes and the firm belief in male superiority, is paramount in the Peruvian culture. Machismo is a point of distinction for a South American male. It creates the image of someone who is strong and respected, in addition to being protective and providing well for his wife and family. There is a persistent double standard in the treatment of men and women. Whereas men may have a mistress or lover, women are strictly forbidden to do this. Whereas a man can divorce his wife because of her adultery, a woman generally cannot do the same unless there is a public scandal.

As it is a Hispanic concept, machismo is not practiced by the native peoples. The Quechua still practice trial marriage, where women and men choose their partners and can end the relationship when they so wish. The woman is free to enter another marriage with no stigma attached to her. Any children resulting from the union are regarded as belonging to the community as a whole.

The 1993 constitution guarantees the equality of women and provides laws that do not discriminate against them. The Domestic Workers Law, passed in 2003, outlines basic rights, such as requiring employers to provide health care. Government enforcement of its own laws has been problematic, however, as statistics show that only 40 percent of domestic helpers are receiving the health care they are entitled to.

A survey by the World Health Organization (WHO) showed that 31 percent of women of middle-and low-income backgrounds in Lima had reported at least one case of physical assault in the previous year. The true figure is likely higher, as many such crimes go unreported due to the fear of further retaliation. Police suspect that only 10 percent of crimes committed against women are reported.

The Truth and Reconciliation Report of 2003 found that former President Alberto Fujimori conducted a program of forced sterilizations against indigenous women during his regime. Under the guise of a public health plan, some three hundred thousand Quechua and Aymara women were coerced into having operations that rendered them unable to get pregnant. The widespread program was aimed at poor women—and to a lesser extent, men—as part of a campaign intended to combat poverty, but human rights organizations have labeled it genocide.

FAMILY

The family is the most important social unit in Peru and forms the center of the community. Singlehood is unusual and deemed unacceptable. There is little socialization between people who are not kin.

A young woman is dressed in traditional bridal attire for the ceremony in the Sacred Valley.

There are regional and socioeconomic differences as to what constitutes a household. However, a group composed of several siblings and their respective spouses is usually the basic domestic unit. Most often children live with their families until they marry and, sometimes, even afterward as well.

The family cycle begins with the marriage. The minimum legal age for both men and women is sixteen. The arrangement can be very flexible for some in the lower classes and the Quechua. Often an alliance between a couple is arranged by their parents, but it is initiated because of the couple's choice. Next they enter a period of *sirvinakuy* (seer-veen-ah-KEE), meaning "to serve each other," during which the woman works with her mother-in-law and the man with his father-in-law. This is a test of their readiness for marriage. During this stage they may sleep together under the same roof, usually with the man's family. The couple generally does not marry until a child is conceived, showing the union to be fruitful, and even then might postpone

the wedding for a long time. Weddings are frequently ornate and expensive occasions that take years to finance.

A patriarchal system exists within the family, where the father is the head of the household. Young men achieve independence from their fathers only gradually over a period of years. Even among brothers, the eldest takes precedence. Boys generally inherit from their fathers and girls from their mothers. As the parents grow older, they usually loosen their authoritative hold on the family.

A wedding procession in Arequipa features ornate traditional costumes.

Migration to urban areas can weaken the ties of rural families, making them less complete and less extended. The migrants are also cut off from a family base. To compensate for this isolation, they move to places where relatives have previously migrated.

Because race is so important in determining one's social class and socioeconomic position, family background or a good family name is one of the key aspects of life. Families descended from the sixteenth century Spanish settlers are more than proud of this fact. If the family has a crest or coat of arms, this is proudly displayed above the door of their home.

GODPARENTS

Social life revolves around the family, and its importance is paramount. To offset this influence and connect the family with the outside world, godparents are chosen for children for the major religious and social events in their lives. Baptism, the first haircut, and marriage are the main events for which they are chosen.

A child might have several sets of godparents during his or her lifetime, but those chosen for baptism are the most important. Having godparents was originally a Hispanic custom, but it is also practiced by the native peoples today.

PATRONAGE

Hispanic countries have a tradition of strong, tight-knit families, and Peru is no exception. In the world of business, this is often extended so that family members are incorporated into firms that may be family-run or publicly owned. Although nepotism is not considered appropriate in North America, such patronage in Peru is seen to be perfectly reasonable.

One of the principal reasons for patronage is that an employer who selects family members for the job knows the strengths and weaknesses of the individuals being hired, often having known them all their lives and perhaps their parents as well. The employer can thus match them to jobs that suit their skills accurately. The employer can also trust family members more than strangers, and the employees in return work to the best of their abilities out of family loyalty. It is considered unthinkable for an employer to look outside his or her family or for somebody not intimately known when hiring.

In some ways the system of patronage is detrimental to business because it can prevent new talents and ideas from entering a firm. It can dissuade more talented people who are not family members from making a positive contribution to the family. Few positions of importance will ever be given to those who are not family members.

Depending on the region in which they live, the duties of godparents vary, but generally when their godchildren are baptized, gifts are given to the parents and children and a contribution is made to a fiesta if the family decides to hold one.

Godparents are meant to give a good start in life to their godchildren, especially in the godchildren's formative years. As a godchild grows up, godparents are less obliged to help in the upbringing of the child unless the child is in serious trouble. It is meant to be a lifelong relationship of great love and respect.

Sometimes when a godchild is orphaned, he or she is raised by a godparent. Social and emotional ties are created, and the serious obligations of the godparent are paid back by the child's love and respect.

People within or outside the family can be chosen as godparents, but generally it is better for a well-off person, a *hacienda* (ranch) owner, boss, or prominent mestizo to be chosen. In the native community this is a way of linking the family to the wider community and society at large.

For the poor it acknowledges their dependence on the rich, and this in turn obliges the rich to better the lot of the less fortunate.

Godchildren call their godfather *padrino* (pah-DREE-no) and their godmother *madrina* (mah-DREE-nah), and the parents of the children call the godparents *compadre* (com-PAH-dray) and *comadre* (com-MAH-dray), respectively. These affectionate names indicate the closeness of the relationship both for the children and for their parents.

HEALTH

People line up for clean water in Pisco after an earthquake in 2007.

Peruvians' health is generally improving, but government health care spending is low. The quality of health care is disproportionately better in Lima and along the coast, where transportation and communication infrastructures are stronger and better established. In 2013, the World Health Organization (WHO) reported that Peru spent $354 per capita annually on health care. For comparison to other South American countries, Chile spent $1,204 per capita, and Brazil spent $1,085. The United States, meanwhile, spent $9,146.

Like other Latin American nations, Peru's public health system faces problems, but is getting better. In 2013, UNICEF estimated that 91 percent of the urban population had access to safe drinking water in their households, while 66 percent of those living in rural areas had the same access. The country's infant mortality rate (meaning the rate of deaths in the first year of life) has decreased in recent decades, from 108 deaths per thousand births in 1970, to 14 in 2012. Routine immunization coverage was very high, close to 100 percent in some cases.

In 2015, the mosquito-borne Zika virus broke out in Peru's neighbor, Brazil, and began spreading throughout South America. Usually, the virus causes only a mild illness, but in pregnant women, it is suspected of causing serious birth defects in the unborn babies. The infants are born with microcephaly, or unusually small heads. Brazilian health authorities reported more than 3,500 microcephaly cases between October 2015 and January 2016. Peru announced its first case of the virus in January 2016.

EDUCATION

A good economy grows out of a well-educated workforce. According to the Peruvian constitution, education is compulsory and free through secondary school. As a result, primary and secondary school enrollment levels have increased greatly. Almost all children enter primary school, though enrollment in secondary school drops off to about 77 percent. Families living in poverty often have little choice but to remove their older children from school so they can work and help feed the family.

In primary school, children are taught mathematics, communications, art, personal development, science and environment, religion, and physical education.

Children attend school on in the floating village of Uros Island in Lake Titicaca.

The Peruvian system breaks down basic education into three cycles, with students proceeding to the next cycle on completion of the previous one. Education is obligatory from ages six to sixteen, during which time students are expected to complete their basic education.

In rural areas lessons in the early years are conducted in the native language, usually Quechua or Aymara. Spanish is taught in the upper grades. Many children live in remote areas far from schools, so a system of *núcleos* (NOO-klay-ohs), which are something like satellite schools, was developed. Scattered throughout the country, *núcleos* serve the needs of several nearby communities. Although the *núcleos* have increased enrollment levels, critics are quick to note that low wages paid by the government have yielded unskilled teachers.

Adult literacy is up from 85.1 percent in 1990 to 94.5 percent in 2014, and even higher for young people. Nevertheless, in 2012, Peru came in last in a ranking of sixty-five participating nations by the Programme for International Student Assessment in student achievement in mathematics, science, and reading.

A VILLAGE IN THE ANDES

The road to a typical village in the Andes is usually narrow and made of earth, baked hard in the summer and turned muddy from torrents of rain in the winter. A network of narrow roads runs over the mountains, connecting small, isolated villages, but in bad weather these roads can be totally impassable. Old buses and heavy trucks use these roads in addition to pack animals such as llamas.

At the end of such a road, the village is mainly inhabited by Quechua who have lived in the same way for a thousand years. The few concessions to modern living are Western dress (for some), running water (which is still rare), metal pots and pans, radios, and flashlights. Some farmers might have an old truck. Crops and livestock introduced by the Spanish have also been adopted.

Electricity is rare, though more and more rural areas are getting hooked up. Some big villages have a generator. A village is likely to have safe drinking water from a few taps dotted throughout the village. If not, people have to trek to the nearest stream or spring several times a day to carry water back.

The crops a village grows depend on the altitude of the village. A village high in the mountains grows potatoes and a few grains and keeps herds of llamas, sheep, goats, and, if they are relatively wealthy, some cattle. On the lower levels, lemons, limes, avocados, and chilies are cultivated in addition to ordinary vegetables. The crops are usually planted from low to high altitude, and harvested in the reverse order.

A Quechua family walks along the road to their home in the high mountain village above the town of Ollantaytambo.

Houses are typically made of earthen bricks baked in the sun or, in rare cases, stone. The dwellings usually have one or two rooms that are roofed with a heavy thatch of puna grasses. The floors are made of hardened earth, and cooking is done in a hearth in the center of the floor. The houses are often smoky from the hearth fire, and the undersides of roofs are black and sooty. There is little furniture beyond a stool or two. A comparatively wealthy family might have a locally made, rough-hewn bed or table. The bed is usually a pallet covered with blankets and sheepskins. In a prosperous home there might be a bed frame with a mattress of bundled reeds.

Women squat on the floor; men sit on benches made from earth. Families own very few personal items: clothing, pots and pans, tools and farming implements, their house, a little land, and, most important, the battery-run radio. People in the Andes begin their day to the sound of the radio. There are hundreds of radio stations in Peru but the one the highlanders listen to is Radio Tawantinsuyu, where DJs speak in Quechua and folk music starts the day. Much of its broadcasting is dedicated to reading personal messages to distant villagers who have no telephone. For people who live in a remote village and only occasionally visit small market towns, a radio is an important connection with the rest of the world.

The woman of the house is the first to rise, stirring last night's embers into a fire and then putting on the kettle to brew some mate (mah-tay), a sort of herbal tea. At breakfast, which is around dawn, mate is served to the family with either mote (MOH-tay), boiled dried corn, or, more rarely, bread.

As the family eats breakfast the mother prepares lunch, or almuerzo (al-MWER-zo), which is eaten when most people in North America would be eating their breakfast. Almuerzo consists of a thick soup of potatoes and other vegetables, a hot sauce made of chilies, and a mug of chicha (CHEE-chah), a beer made of fermented corn. This meal is served to all the workers in the household, who would usually gather in the kitchen. These might include fathers, sons, and grandfathers. There may also be godparents of their children or just neighbors who owe the family a day's work in return for the family's earlier labor in their fields. After eating, the men go to the fields and work steadily throughout the day. In order to complete the tasks before nightfall, they will only take occasional breaks.

When the men have left, the mother begins to prepare the third meal of the day, which is more complex and plentiful than the other two. It includes two or three dishes with the usual potatoes and mote, but with the addition of meat as a special thanks to the men helping her family.

If the job the men are carrying out in the field is a communal one, the woman may be assisted in her task by the wives or mothers of the field hands. She is also expected to look after the children, milk the cow, lead it to pasture, and feed the chickens and pigs.

Around noon she packs the meal with all the utensils, plates, spoons, and maybe a bottle or two of trago *(TRAH-goh), a cane liquor, and chicha, and leaves for the fields with the children and other women. After the men have eaten and drunk their fill, they return to work.*

*The women will either sit and watch while drinking chicha and playing with the children, or they will work in the fields themselves, plowing, hoeing, or reaping. The children drink an unfermented and sweetened chicha that comes in two flavors—*chichi blanca, *made from white corn, and* chicha morada, *made from purple corn.*

At the end of the day, which is usually twilight, everything is gathered up and they all go home. Cattle, sheep, or goats are herded up and taken back also. At home they drink a last cup of chicha before the beds are laid out. The fire is reduced to a few glowing embers that will light the next day's kindling, and the family goes to bed.

INTERNET LINKS

www.theguardian.com/global-development/2016/jan/04/peru-forced-sterilisation-quipu-project-alberto-fujimori
This article highlights the forced sterilization of poor people during the Fujimori administration.

www.peruthisweek.com/news
This English-language site gives insight into various modern lifestyles in Peru.

www.smithsonianmag.com/travel/weaving-women-ausangate-peru-textiles-tradition-quechua-identity-180956468/?no-ist
This article focuses on the women weavers of the Southern Andes.

www.unicef.org/infobycountry/peru_statistics.html
Detailed health and education statistics for Peru are available on this UNICEF site.

RELIGION

The Monastery of Saint Francis in the Historic Center of Lima dates from 1673 and is on the UNESCO World Heritage List.

8

A S IS TRUE IN MOST OF LATIN America, Roman Catholicism is the primary religion of Peru. While the country doesn't have an official religion, its constitution does state that "the government recognizes the Catholic Church as an important element in the historical, cultural, and moral formation of Peru and lends it its cooperation." In other words, although the constitution grants freedom of religion, the government gives special consideration to the Catholic Church.

To many indigenous Peruvians, however, the majestic mountains that surround them have spirits. People make offerings to the earth, and images of the sun figure prominently in their religious iconography. Nevertheless, these same people consider themselves to be Catholics. For the people of the Andes, Incan beliefs and Catholic doctrine have fused into a harmonious whole in which the festival of Saint John the Baptist conveniently coincides with the old Incan festival for the winter solstice, and traditional marriage customs naturally accommodate a church wedding.

Although Peru is overwhelmingly Catholic, some people display only nominal allegiance to the church. Only 15 percent of Peruvian Roman Catholics attend mass weekly. Most people practice "popular

The Convento de San Francisco (Monastery of Saint Francis) is an important religious complex in Lima made up of the cathedral, the convent, and two other churches, La Soledad and El Milagro. The convent houses a world-renowned library of antique books. In 1943, catacombs filled with thousands of skulls and bones, passageways, and crypts were discovered under the cathedral.

Catholicism," which means occasionally attending special events like the sacraments, festivals, processions, or saints' days. Among the middle and upper classes, religion is losing its importance. Some are alienated by the church's policies, such as opposition to birth control.

ANCIENT PERUVIAN BELIEFS

The religion of the ancient Incas permeated all aspects of public and private life. They worshipped many gods, goddesses, and spirits, each of which was responsible for a different aspect of life.

Viracocha was the most important god, having created the sun, moon, stars, earth, oceans, and weather—in fact, all natural things. Like many Incan gods, Viracocha is neither male nor female, nor just one being. The god's complexity is apparent when one considers his or her responsibility both for water and fire.

Illapa was another important god representing thunderbolts, lightning, rain, hail, snow, and frost. He was venerated mainly in the highlands. Together with his son and his brother, they were depicted as the deities of the mountains.

The god Pachacamac ruled over the lowlands and the underworld, causing earthquakes and pestilence. He was represented as a golden fox. Another god was Amaru, a serpent who rose from the underworld. Amaru symbolized the communication between the living and the dead.

Some deities were exclusively female. These included Killa, the moon, who was the wife of the sun. Statues of her were made of silver, and those of the sun were of gold. Killa was associated with the earth and death.

The center of the Incan religion was undoubtedly the sun god, Inti. Although not as powerful as Viracocha, the sun was more physical and less mystical.

The emperors at Cuzco demanded to be recognized as direct descendants of the sun. It was believed that this exalted lineage would give them a semidivine status, as well as an excuse for military subjugation of other regions. After all, the sun reigned over the highlands (considered the center of the empire) and the heavens. He was viewed as a paternalistic god who

THE NAZCA LINES

In the Nazca Desert in the south of Peru, hundreds of huge drawings, or geoglyphs, are inscribed in the ground. Scholars believe these Nazca Lines, as they are called, were created by the Nazca culture between 500 BCE and 500 CE. The lines cover such a wide area that they are only properly visible from the air. Several dozen figures, mostly animals, but also some humans, are represented: a 600-foot (183 m) lizard, a 300-foot (90 m) monkey with a tightly curled tail, and a condor with a 400-foot (122 m) wingspan.

The lines were created by removing the top layer of earth to reveal the lighter-colored dust beneath. Other designs include geometric shapes and straight lines that run across the desert. The longest line is

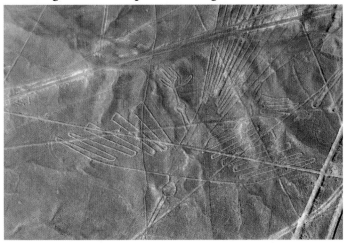

more than 5.5 miles (over 9 km) long. The lines have remained intact over thousands of years due to the site's isolation and the dry, windless climate of the plateau.

Researchers are uncertain as to the purpose of the earthwork art, but most believe the figures are probably religious in nature. Some think they might have served a purpose related to astronomy or cosmology. Others have put forward alternative theories. In 1995, UNESCO added the site to the World Cultural Heritage List. In 2006, a Japanese university research team found one hundred new designs on the site, and then in 2011, discovered two more.

planned for the welfare of the universe and its people, the Incas, while controlling their every action.

THE ROMAN CATHOLIC CHURCH

Peru is a predominantly Catholic country, with 81 percent of the population professing to be Roman Catholic. Evangelical Christians account for 12.5 percent, and other religions 3.3 percent. Around 2.9 percent do not claim a faith or are atheist or agnostic. Often Catholicism is combined with native myths and legends. Catholic festivals were usually substituted for the Incan religious festivals on the same date, so the two inevitably became mixed. The Incan religion and other native religions linger on in the mountains and jungles. This synthesis of Catholicism and pre-Columbian practices is called "popular religion."

Peru's history and destiny have been profoundly shaped by the Roman Catholic Church. The church reached Peru with Francisco Pizarro in 1533, and a few years later, in 1537, the diocese of Cuzco was established. The church quickly founded hospitals, including a twelve-room hospital in Lima for natives, and built schools. Almost sixty schools were established by 1548, and in 1551 the University of San Marcos in Lima was created.

Schools were part of the church's campaign to convert the natives. This method started immediately with the Spanish arrival. Many obstacles, including the varied forms of local cults and the inaccessibility of the native population, made this conversion difficult.

Although they were the prime target of conversion, native peoples were excluded from becoming priests until the seventeenth century. Mestizos and Creoles (a person of European descent who was born in Spanish America) made up the majority of the clergy. Foreign priests from Spain and elsewhere in Latin America have often been needed because of a dramatic decline in the number of priests since the nineteenth century. Until as recently as 1963, 70 percent of bishops were foreign. In 1821 there was one priest for every five hundred people. Today there is one priest for every ten thousand people.

The seventeenth century was known as the religious century. The church was at the pinnacle of the artistic and intellectual culture it had helped to

Peru is the birthplace of two saints of particular importance to the Americas: Saint Rose of Lima and Saint Martin de Porres.

Saint Martin de Porres was born in Lima in 1579, the illegitimate son of a noble Spaniard and a black woman. It was not customary at that time to allow a mulatto to enter a religious order in Peru, but because of his exceptional qualities and virtue he was admitted to the Dominican Order in 1610. Martin was known for his kindness to all people, especially to the poor and the unfortunate. He was also a special friend to animals. He established an orphanage and a school for the youth of Lima, which is considered his monument. His feast day is November 5.

Saint Rose of Lima was the first person born in the New World to be canonized by the Catholic Church and is called the patron saint of the Americas and the Philippines. She was born in Lima in 1586. Although her mother wanted her to marry, Rose was determined to devote her life to religion, and in 1606 her mother relented and Rose became a nun, living in seclusion in a hut on the family property. Her feast day is August 30.

create. Many sculptures, paintings, and the grand colonial cathedrals were all made at the behest of the church. Two saints were also canonized during this period, the most famous being Santa Rosa (Saint Rose) of Lima (1586—1617). The first saint to be canonized in the Americas, her sympathy for the native peoples made her Peru's originator of social services. Another Peruvian saint, San Martín (Saint Martin) de Porres (1579—1639) was the first black saint. A district in Lima is named after him.

CHURCH AND STATE

The church in Peru has always been involved in social matters, which has occasionally conflicted with the state's interest. Formerly, priests often told people how they ought to vote. During the campaign for independence in the 1800s, the clergy (mainly consisting of mestizos) supported the revolutionaries against the Spanish.

In 1845 Catholicism was made the official state religion. Foreigners were permitted to conduct their own services, but no Peruvians were allowed to

SHAMANISM: MAGIC AND CURE

Shamanism has been popular for over three thousand years. As a developing country, most of Peru's population cannot afford or even have access to doctors or proper medical care. Many people, especially the natives and the poor, rely on the shaman's ancient healing art or curandero *(kur-ahn-DAIR-oh), the rural spiritual healer. Even former President Fernando Belaúnde's family employed one. The shaman can be found in every large community, principally in the Sierra and the Selva. People may travel hundreds of miles to see one. The people of the Amazon region have best maintained the shamanistic culture and spiritual traditions.*

Shamanism uses herbs and hands-on therapy to cure people not just from physical sickness but from fear, jealousy, tension, and anger. The treatment draws on the combined spiritual and magical elements of native culture. It attempts to treat one's overall wellness rather than just the symptoms of illnesses.

Most shamans use hallucinogens (potent drugs extracted from plants) that the Incas previously used. Under the hallucinogen's influence, a patient experiences revelation, a period when the shaman asks the person questions and sets tasks that are interpreted to reveal the source of the illness. Shamans also consume the drug themselves in order to see into the future, recover lost souls, and find lost objects. Sometimes the whole community participates. Traditional spirit-songs are sung to enable them to get in touch with the ancestors' spirit world. In a way the shaman acts as a conserving force against the discordances of modern life and the encroaching industrial world, preserving a tribe's culture as established by their ancestors.

attend. The 1920 constitution gave individuals freedom of religion, which was subsequently reaffirmed in the 1979 constitution. In the constitution of 1933 and in amendments made in 1940 and 1961, the state declared that the country was no longer officially or formally Roman Catholic. Despite this, the church was given special status, and religious instruction is still obligatory in all educational institutions in the country.

Although it has been one of the more conservative churches in Latin America, the Peruvian church has increasingly supported socially progressive movements and has proposed reforms. A consequence has been an increase in the church's popularity with the poor. When the late Pope John Paul II visited in 1985 and 1988, vast public rallies were held in celebration.

In 2014, President Ollanta Humala invited Pope Francis to visit Peru, but when the pope toured parts of Latin America in 2015, he did not stop there. Francis said he hopes to visit his native Argentina, as well as Chile and Uruguay, in 2016. He has also promised to visit Peru at some point in the future.

INTERNET LINKS

www.catholic.org/saints/saint.php?saint_id=306
This site provides information about Saint Martin de Porres.

www.catholic.org/saints/saint.php?saint_id=446
Read a biography of Saint Rose of Lima on this site.

www.limaeasy.com/culture-guide/historical-churches
This site highlights some of the most important churches and cathedrals in Lima.

pulitzercenter.org/reporting/peru-conundrum-pope-environmental-message-divides-his-people
This article highlights Peru's mixed reception of Pope Francis's environmental message.

LANGUAGE

NO SUBAS A
LOS MUROS

DON'T CLIMB
UP OVER
THE WALLS

A wooden sign at the site of the Pisac Inca Ruins advises visitors in Spanish and English.

9

THE SPANISH LANGUAGE IS probably Spain's greatest export. When the Spanish conquistadors conquered South America in the sixteenth century, they planted the New World land with the Old World language, and its roots took a firm hold. The Spanish language quickly rose to prominence in Peru. Native peoples were accustomed to having rulers who spoke a different language. Indeed, the Spanish conquest was helped by the fact that the Incan emperors and their court at Cuzco spoke a different language from their subjects, who thus felt little allegiance to them.

Nearly all the countries in Latin America use Spanish as their official or main language, with the exception of Brazil, where Portuguese is spoken. After including the population of Spain and Spanish speakers in North America, there are more than four hundred million Spanish speakers today. Spanish is the world's second most popular language, after Mandarin, and is spoken in thirty-one countries.

Today, Spanish, Quechua, and Aymara are all official languages of Peru. People of the highlands generally speak Quechua or Aymara, and the native peoples of the Amazon region speak languages from twelve different linguistic families. In addition to these language variations, there is also Creole slang. Linguistically varied and used at all levels of society, Creole slang is a result of the rich mixture of cultural influences Peru has incorporated.

NATIVE LANGUAGES

Aymara is a regional language with few speakers, most of whom live around the southernmost part of Peru adjacent to Lake Titicaca. In comparison, many native people still speak Quechua, the ancient language of the Incas. It is popularly known to the native peoples as *Runasimi*, meaning "Mouth of the People." During the days of the Incan empire, it was spoken in the region that is modern-day Peru, Bolivia, Ecuador, and parts of Argentina and Chile. It continued to spread even after the Spanish invasion, but its use declined and is now confined to Peru and parts of Ecuador and Bolivia.

There are around eight to ten million Quechua speakers in South America. Many are from the Andean highlands. It is the largest indigenous language to survive in the Americas and has given some words to the English language: *llama*, *cóndor*, *puma*, and *pampa*, among others.

Quechua has many regional varieties, a result of the immensity of the old Incan empire, which encompassed many different peoples. The purest and most prestigious form of Quechua is now spoken around Cuzco, the former capital of the Incas.

For a long time, Quechua was seen as a backward language or a language of subversion. It was outlawed by the Spanish in 1780 after a peasant revolt, and it was even discouraged by Simón Bolívar. Despite this, it survived.

The Incas did not have a written language or alphabet. Instead they had *quipu* (KEE-poo), an elaborate system of knotted string. This simple system was effective in communicating complex pieces of information (including detailed censuses) used in administering a large empire.

During the sixteenth century the Spanish clergy tried to learn Quechua, so that they could record the Incas' past history and also convert the natives by translating the Bible into a common language that would be understood.

They wrote Quechua in the Roman alphabet, and it has been written this way ever since. The first book that was printed in Peru was a catechism in Quechua, which the priests used to teach the natives.

GREETINGS AND GESTURES

Men and women shake hands when meeting and parting. Men embrace close friends or pat them on the back. Women kiss one another on the cheek. When two women are introduced, they may kiss one another. The same is sometimes true of men and women. Elders and officials are greeted with their title and last name. Principal titles are *doctor*, *profesor*, *arquitecto* (ahr-kee-TEC-toh), or architect, and *ingeniero* (een-hain-YER-oh), which means engineer. Some Peruvians call foreigners *gringo* if a man or *gringa* if a woman. In Peru this is a normal form of address.

People discuss family and occupation when meeting someone. To rush in and talk about business is considered rude. Some topics of conversation can be difficult. Because of the recent political situation in Peru, politics can be a very touchy area. Another sensitive topic relates to a person's ancestry. Most Peruvians feel more comfortable being associated with their Spanish colonial background than their native heritage.

When Peruvians converse, they stand much closer to one another than people in the United States do. To back away is taken as an insult.

This sixteenth-century illustration shows an Inca accountant and his quipu strings.

THE PRESS

The 1993 constitution guarantees media freedom. This upholds the right to information, opinion, expression, and dissemination of thought in any form and through any medium without prior authorization or censorship. However, this is not always upheld in practice. Although outright censorship is not

SOME BASIC WORDS IN SPANISH AND QUECHUA

ENGLISH	SPANISH	QUECHUA
one	uno	hoq
two	dos	iskay
three	tres	kinsa
four	cuatro	tawa
five	cinco	pisqa
six	seis	soqta
seven	siete	qanchis
eight	ocho	pusaq
nine	nueve	isqon
ten	diez	chunka
good morning	buenos días	rimay kullaiki tutamanta
good evening	buenas noches	rimay kullaiki kaituta
yes	sí	ari
no	no	manan
hello	¡hola!	napaykullayki!
please	por favor	ama jina kaychu
thank you	muchas gracias	anchata sulpaiky
how are you?	¿cómo está usted?	allinllachu
fine	bien	allinllan

officially in place, journalists are routinely subjected to political pressure, lawsuits, physical attacks, and outright murder.

Peru has suffered from a long history of political interferences in the media. In 1974 the Peruvian press was nationalized, which immediately stopped critical reporting about the government. The papers were returned to private ownership in 1980, but the previous six years of government control had drastically damaged their quality. Escalating political violence in the 1980s caused civilian governments to once again exert pressure on the press to subdue reports, and the latter even excluded references to terrorism.

In 1990 the Fujimori government closed *El Diario*, considering it a supporter of the terrorist Sendero Luminoso. Between 1983 and 1991 numerous journalists were killed, seventeen of them by government security forces.

Today's record is no better: the National Association of Journalists of Peru (ANP) recorded forty-seven attacks against journalists and media outlets in just four months—January through April—in 2014. According to the Peruvian Press Council, the murders of fifty-eight journalists between 1982 and 2011 remain unsolved.

Colorful newspapers fill a news stand in Cuzco.

INTERNET LINKS

www.ancient.eu/Quipu
This is a quick overview of the knot-recording system of the Inca.

freedomhouse.org/report/freedom-press/2015/peru
This organization ranks countries according to their press and media freedom.

www.omniglot.com/writing/quechua.htm
This site gives a basic introduction to the Quechuan language.

ARTS

Ceramic Pucara bulls are traditionally handcrafted roof ornaments commonly seen on buildings throughout southern Peru.

10

P ERU HAS MANY CULTURES. Thousands of years before the Europeans arrived, pre—Columbian New World civilizations such as the Andes Incas came and went in the area that is now Peru. Over the centuries many civilizations contributed to a diverse, dynamic, and thriving culture. Racial and geographic factors produced a regionalism in the arts: the Amazonian natives retain their cultural independence, the urbanized coast is greatly influenced by Europe, whereas the Sierra still preserves the flavor of the Incan empire. Probably the only area of artistic expression that all of Peru's people share is the art inspired by the Catholic Church.

"Peru is for me a kind of incurable disease and my feeling for her is intense, bitter, and full of the violence that characterizes passion."
—Mario Vargas Llosa (b. 1936), Peruvian writer, politician, journalist, college professor, and Nobel Prize winner.

NATIVE AND SPANISH: TWO SEPARATE ARTS

Peru's artistic achievements fall into four periods: pre-Incan, Incan, colonial, and postcolonial. There was little disruption between the pre-Incan and Incan periods, but colonization brought increasing tension and division in the artistic world between the traditional native cultures and the new. The Spanish conquerors destroyed much of the artwork created by the Incas. Nearly all the metalwork done in gold or silver was melted down. The Spanish imposed their own culture, destroying native art and traditions. For centuries after the conquest, the arts were little more than a direct imitation of Spanish styles. Ironically, the church often employed native artisans to carve statues and decorate interiors.

After independence from Spain, Creoles tried to forge a new artistic culture distinct from the Spanish as well as from the native culture. They began to look toward the whole of Europe rather than just to Spain. It was only in the early twentieth century that Peruvians began to appreciate their full artistic heritage. In present-day Peru, European influences and the indigenous past remain as two separate, often conflicting artistic strands.

FROM POTTERY TO PAINTING

Some of the earliest remains of visual art in Peru are found in the pottery and weaving of ancient cultures. Many different civilizations, such as the Chavín, Paracas, Nazca, Chimu, and Mochica, developed new techniques and styles that they passed on to the next culture. To this day, the designs and colors from the pottery and textiles of ancient civilizations are used and made in a similar way. Their bright colors make modern masonry and architecture seem dull in comparison. Typical motifs include many fish, reptiles, birds, and mammals. The Mochica culture introduced the representation of everyday human experience: children playing, someone with a toothache, women washing, and lots of portraits.

Military expansion facilitated the spread of artistic styles; with the rise of the Incan empire, its artistic styles became universalized. The Incas incorporated many earlier designs in their work and spread these throughout their empire.

With the coming of the Spanish, painting with oils on canvas and fresco painting were introduced. Churches and monasteries required decorations and paintings; at first these were imported from Spain. Soon European painters arrived, especially from Italy. One of the first was Bernardo Bitti, who emigrated to Peru in 1548.

In the late nineteenth century, artists began to rediscover their native past. The *costumbrista* (kos-toom-BREE-stah) movement made the everyday life of the native peoples the subject of art. Painters such as José Sebogal tried to create a national school based on native themes.

In the twentieth century, visual artists were divided into two schools: the *indigenistas* (een-dee-hain-EES-tahs), who followed the native culture and style, and the *hispanistas* (ees-pan-EES-tahs), who drew on the Spanish heritage. Some Peruvian artists have tried to combine the two. Fernando de Szyszlo (b. 1925) is the best-known contemporary artist to include native motifs in his abstract painting. Ricardo Grau and Macedonio de la Torre incorporate the traditions of their country with modern European styles.

Peru's most famous modern sculptor, Joaquín Roca Rey (1923–2004), worked in metals and had exhibitions all over the world. His work is exhibited in various museums in the United States and Lima.

This painting of the Virgin Mary was made by a Peruvian follower of Bernardo Bitti around the year 1600.

THE BRILLIANCE OF INCAN GOLDSMITHS

The quantity of gold that came from Peru in the sixteenth century was colossal, and most of it was originally in the form of art objects that the Spanish then melted down into ingots. The chronicler Garcilaso de la Vega describes the Emperor Atahualpa's gardens as including life-size imitations of corn, flowers, and animals, all made in gold and silver. Whole buildings and courts were sheathed in plates of gold. Yet nothing, no matter how beautiful, was spared by the Spanish. The examples that survive today are extremely

An embossed gold vase from the Chimu civilization predates the Inca culture.

rare and come from remote regions of the Incan Empire or from looted graves. Gold was a sacred element. To the Incas it symbolized power and was often used as a tribute to the emperor or buried with nobles. Items buried included images of gods, cups, jewelry, and ornaments.

The tools used to make these objects were primitive, consisting mainly of stone hammers, chisels, and wood and stone rollers for smoothing. Decorative techniques included incising, stamping, scratching, and inlaying with precious metals such as silver and gold, expensive gems such as turquoise and emeralds, as well as amber. The artwork that is preserved in Peru's museums today highlights the astounding craftsmanship and high social standing accorded to craftsworkers in Incan times.

ARCHITECTURE

Before the Incas, buildings were constructed mainly of mud and straw bricks and some wood. Even today many poor people live in mud and straw adobe houses. The artistry of the Incas is visible in their architecture. Incan architecture is technically very accomplished, as can be seen in structures like the walls in Cuzco and the great city of Machu Picchu. Massive blocks of rock were crafted with stone or bronze tools, smoothed off with sand, and then dragged up and down the many steep mountains of Peru using human strength alone. The Incas covered the walls of their dwellings with gold; decorations, statues, and ornaments filled alcoves.

With the arrival of the Spanish, a new style of architecture emerged, which included new types of buildings, such as churches and monasteries. The Spanish relied on native workers and materials, but they created a very Spanish style. Mansions in Lima were replicas of Andalusian structures. Also

evident are the Moorish origins of the Spanish style. One of the most ornate churches in Peru is La Compañía in Cuzco. Its magnificent baroque facade rivals the splendor of the city's cathedral.

Native influences slowly began to seep into architectural style and decorations. Incan motifs, such as the sun and pumas, can often be found in church friezes. Such native touches can be seen in many buildings in the more remote areas, especially Puno and Cajamarca.

MUSIC AND DANCE

Peru's music does not fit into one category. The multitude of different regions, histories, ethnicities, and classes has ensured a wide variety of sounds.

The most well-known Peruvian music is the Andean folk music originally played in the highlands. Sad songs are mixed with whooping, energetic ones, and all are performed to a communal and stylized dance.

Andean folk music dates back to the ancient civilizations of Peru. Clay panpipes have been found in ancient graveyards on the coast. The Incas

The ornate façade of the *Iglesia de La Compañía* (Church of the Company) is considered a masterpiece of the churrigueresque, a style of extravagant architectural ornamentation that began in seventeenth-century Spain.

used a variety of flutes and panpipes, conch-shell trumpets, and drums made from puma skin. The Spanish introduced stringed instruments, which the native musicians adapted. Some uniquely Andean instruments used in folk music are the *charango* (chah-RAHN-go), a kind of mandolin using an armadillo shell as a sound box, and the Andean harp. Other standard instruments in folk bands are cane flutes, panpipes, and drums.

Peñas, or nightclubs, can be smart and chic or untidy and primitive, but either way they are home to *criolla* (cree-OH-yah),or Creole-style music. Spanish guitars and percussion instruments blend music from many sources, African to European, to create an often slow, romantic form with love ballads. There are regional variations with their own accompanying dances.

Chicha music, named after the beer, developed in Colombia. It is faster than criolla and mixes saucy lyrics with energetic percussion and electric guitar backing. Chicha can often be heard in the highlands but is heard mainly in the jungle, where it is played at many Saturday night fiestas.

A style that shows the diversity of Peruvian music is *música negra* (MOO-see-kah NAY-grah), or "black music." This style originated in the old slave communities on the coast. The music is associated with social protest and portrays daily life in the communities.

A musician in Pisac plays traditional panpipes.

LITERATURE

The written word has a relatively recent place in Peruvian history. The Incas had no system of writing, although literature abounded in myths and legends that were passed on orally. The Spanish conquest generated the first pieces of a national literature, mainly historical and descriptive accounts about the conquest. The *Royal Commentaries of the Incas* (1609) is a fascinating

THE WEAVERS OF THE ANDES

One of the most iconic of Peruvian arts and crafts is created in the Andes Mountains by indigenous women. Weaving has been a vital part of Peruvian culture for thousands of years, passed along through countless generations of Quechua people. In high altitude rural communities, women, and also some men, weave the blankets, ponchos, belts, hats, and other items that have become treasured worldwide.

The weavers use the highly prized alpaca wool, but also llama wool and cotton to create vibrant textiles on simple backstrap looms. The artisans use local materials to make the brightly colored dyes and incorporate symbols and patterns into their textiles that date to Incan times. It can take some five hundred hours, over a period of months, to spin, dye, and weave a traditional Peruvian poncho.

Today, many Andean women are part of weaving cooperatives that help them market their wares to tourists and the outside world. This way, the weavers earn a living while preserving an essential part of their culture.

document providing many insights into the world of the Incas and the Spanish conquest of Peru. It was written by the Inca Garcilaso de la Vega (not to be confused with the Spanish poet of the same name), who was the son of a conquistador and an Incan princess.

Peruvian writing came into its own only in the past few decades. In previous centuries Peruvian writers had reflected the tastes and forms of Spanish literature. The internationally renowned poet César Vallejo (1892–1938) was

Mario Vargas Llosa (b. 1936) is Peru's most famous intellectual and novelist. In 2010, he was awarded the Nobel Prize in Literature.

He first achieved fame in the 1960s when the Mexican writer Carlos Fuentes and the Colombian writer Gabriel García Márquez also came to prominence. Like most Latin American writers, Vargas Llosa has also been active in politics.

With seventeen novels, four plays, an abundance of essays, and the first part of his autobiography, A Fish in the Water, *to his name, Vargas Llosa is a prolific author. Born to an affluent family in Arequipa in 1936, he was sent to school at the Military College in Lima at the age of ten. His first novel,* The Time of the Hero, *deals with the effects of the college's cruel and authoritarian regime on its pupils. The Peruvian military burned the book.*

Although he is a native Peruvian, Vargas Llosa spent many years abroad— mostly in Europe—returning only to spend the summer months at his coastal home near Lima. However, he retained a keen interest in Peruvian politics, and his views changied as he grew older. Initially holding views of the radical left in the 1960s, he gradually moved to the right. Disagreeing with the nationalization of the banks in 1987, he joined a new right-wing political party called Libertad *("Freedom"), which later became the Democratic Front. With its help, he began his bid for the presidency, espousing a radical, free-market economic program that would privatize all of Peru's state companies.*

The writer who had once written so sensitively about his own country was not the politician who entered the 1990 presidential race. Critics said Vargas Llosa seemed very remote from the problems of the Peruvian poor. On a second ballot, he was beaten by Alberto Fujimori. He became a Spanish citizen and now lives in London and Madrid. He acquired Spanish citizenship in 1993, but maintains his Peruvian citizenship as well.

one of the first of a generation of poets, artists, and writers to attempt to free himself from European influence and produce a distinctive voice, even though he lived abroad for many years. Many of Peru's modern artists, poets, writers, and intellectuals still have to go abroad to discover what is unique about their own country. Through a study of foreign styles, they became more aware of their country's individuality. Vallejo and his contemporaries dealt with themes such as the problems of cultural identity and showed an interest in the Incan heritage.

Peru has also produced good modern novelists in addition to the famous Mario Vargas Llosa. Lesser known but equally important are Ciro Alegría, whose *Broad and Alien Is the World* describes life in the Sierra, and Manuel Scorza, whose *Drums for Runas*, written in the style of the South American magic realist school, deals with the struggles of the miners in the highlands. José María Arguedas was uncommon among Peruvian writers because he wrote solely about the native peoples.

INTERNET LINKS

www.artnews.com/2013/03/21/what-makes-peruvian-art-peruvian
Masterpieces of Peruvian art spanning three millennia are featured, with large photographs, on this review of a recent museum exhibition.

www.festival.si.edu/2015/peru/music-of-peru/smithsonian
Smithsonian Folkways presents a comprehensive overview of Peruvian folk music with audio links.

science.nationalgeographic.com/science/archaeology/lost-inca-gold
This article presents the story of lost Incan gold.

www.timetravelturtle.com/2014/09/womens-weaving-cooperative-peru
See beautiful photos of Andean weavers and their crafts on this site.

LEISURE

Paragliders add to the breathtaking scenery in Miraflores.

11

EVERYONE NEEDS SOME DOWN TIME. Even the hardest working people—and in Peru, that probably describes most people—need time to connect with friends and family. In rural areas, Peruvian women may spend their little bit of free time knitting or doing small tasks around the house. Men may enjoy a relaxing meal or spend time drinking chicha with friends. Otherwise, about the only time to relax is during fiestas, when everyone spends the day dancing, eating, and partying.

City dwellers are likely to take a trip to the beach or go to a movie. During the Peruvian summer months, from January to April, they flock to seaside resort towns such as Pucusana and La Isla. A favorite pastime is to spend the evening in a peña—lively nightclubs with colorful performances—dancing, listening to Creole music, and enjoying drinks and food, such as *ceviche*, a popular seafood. Barranco, a suburb of Lima, is particularly well known for its *peñas*.

Sports have always been a good way of bringing a community together, and in small villages, the reward after a hard day's work is often found in playing on the local soccer team. The Incas played versions of badminton and basketball, which are illustrated on ancient vases. Today, Peruvians enjoy baseball, basketball, bowling, and playing

Bullfighting was brought to Peru by none other than the Spanish conquistador Francisco Pizarro. He brought the first Spanish fighting bull, the *toro de lidia*, to Lima, and held the first bullfight in the Americas in 1538.

Boys play soccer in a village along the Amazon River.

pool. Many country clubs offer golf, swimming, and tennis. Volleyball and polo also have a large following (the women's volleyball team won a silver medal at the 1988 Olympics), and even the English game of cricket is played at the Lima Cricket Club. However, these are the sports for people who can afford them. Recreation facilities for everyone are more plentiful in the cities than in the country.

SOCCER

Soccer, called *fútbol*, is the favorite sport in Peru today. Soccer was first played in Lima in 1892. It was introduced by British immigrants, and the first club was founded in 1897, with leagues starting in 1912. The Estadio Nacional (National Stadium) in Lima, which seats forty-five thousand spectators, hosts the most important soccer matches and events. The national team is one of the ten members of the South American Football Confederation. Its nickname is La Blanquirroja ("the white and red"), for the colors of the Peruvian flag. Peruvian football fans are known for their distinctive chant "*¡Arriba Perú!*"

("Come on Peru!"). The team, however, has not played consistently. It qualified for the 1982 World Cup in Spain but has failed to qualify ever since.

Things may be looking up. Peru came third in Chile at the 2015 Copa América, the main international tournament for South American national teams, and was set to participate in the 2016 Centennial Copa América in June 2016 in the United States, and the 2016—2017 qualification matches for the 2018 World Cup finals in Russia.

BEACHES AND WATER SPORTS

The Peruvian coast has a large number of beaches with excellent surfing conditions. Legend has it the sport dates to pre-Incan times, and images found on ancient pottery seem to support that notion. Certainly Peru now enjoys an international reputation among surfers, and has produced a number of world surfing champions.

The most fashionable and famous beaches lie south of Lima. Their vibrant nightlife makes them the favorite haunts of young Peruvians. Yachting is a

A surfer rides a wave at the Punta Hermosa beach in 2015.

popular pastime, even for lower-income Peruvians, with many sailing to the Galapagos Islands some 1,250 miles (2,000 km) away. Deep-sea fishing is popular all along the western coast, where the catch includes black marlin, flounder, sea bass, snook, corvina, and mackerel. In the Andean lakes, fly-fishing for trout is extremely popular, and many tourists come from Europe and the United States to try their luck.

COCKFIGHTING

Cockfighting, which is illegal in most of the United States, is very much the spectator sport of choice among the poor. Trained cocks are placed face to face in a pit or on a stage and let loose to fight each other. The birds are fitted with sharp spurs on their legs, which they use to attack the opponent until one is killed or becomes unable to fight. There are three types of cockfights: the single battle in which two cocks fight; the main battle, where cocks are paired and play an elimination game; and the battle royal, in which several cocks fight each other until only one is standing. The Coliseo de Gallos in Lima hosts fights on most weekends.

Like bullfighting, cockfighting has attracted a chorus of opposition from animal rights proponents who see the activity as a cruel blood sport. In 2012,

Two beautiful roosters prepare to battle it out, probably to the death.

opponents presented sixty thousand signatures to legislators in Peru's lower house, calling for a parliamentary debate on the abolition of sports that mistreated animals for entertainment. The lawmakers refused to back the appeal. It seems cockfighting will remain an important expression of Peru's culture for some time to come.

MOUNTAINEERING AND HIKING

Blessed with majestic mountains, Peru naturally offers great opportunities for climbing and hiking. Thirty-three peaks rise well above 20,000 feet (6,096 m), including Huascaran, Peru's highest. Mountaineers say the Cordillera Blanca, in the Ancash region of Peru, is a climber's paradise; and many people say it's the most beautiful range in the Andes. In particular, Alpamayo is a popular destination. This peak, a steep and distinctive pyramid of ice and snow, was once voted the most beautiful mountain in the world.

In Arequipa, the most popular climb is El Misti, a volcano that dominates the city. However, in 2015, volcanologists said the mountain is beginning to show more signs of seismic activity. If El Misti erupts, it will be the first time since the fifteenth century.

As a tradition, bullfighting came to Peru from Spain at the time of conquest. Today some 540 bullfights take place every year in Peru, more than in any other Latin American country. It is a sport (though some dispute that) associated with old-world glamour, machismo, and derring-do, and it's also practiced in Spain, Colombia, Ecuador, Venezuela, in parts of Mexico, and in southern parts of France.

The oldest bullfighting ring in the Americas, the Plazo de Acho, is in Lima. Built in 1765, the wood and adobe structure is still in use today. In fact, it hosts Peru's largest bullfighting event, the Feria Taurina del Señor de los Milagros, a festival for the "Lord of the Miracles."

A typical bullfight begins with a procession of the toreros *("bullfighters")—the matadors and their assistants—the* picadors *on horseback, and the* banderilleros *on foot—all wearing traditional costumes. The bull is released into the arena and the matador confronts and provokes it by waving his cape. A picador with a lance stabs the bull behind the neck, to weaken and enrage it. Then, the banderilleros stab the bull in the shoulders with sharp, barbed sticks decorated with brightly colored ribbons. In the final stage of the action, the matador faces the bull alone, armed with a small red cape and a sword.*

The matador, using elegant poses and skilled flourishes of the cape, choreographs his interaction with the bull. He moves the animal through a series of passes, closer and closer to him. Finally he plunges his sword into the bull, aiming for its heart or aorta for a fast kill. If the matador succeeds on his first try, he is cheered. If the spectators are pleased, they wave white handkerchiefs and the matador is awarded one of the bull's ears. Frequently, however, the first stab misses its mark and the matador must try again and again. Meanwhile, the bull vomits blood and dies a slow, agonizing death.

Bullfighting remains popular in Peru despite rising opposition worldwide. Critics decry the event as a vicious blood sport in which cruelty to animals is demonstrated for entertainment. In 2012, Panama banned bullfighting. Three states in Mexico have banned it and even some parts of Spain have outlawed the practice. Some places, such as Costa Rica, only allow a non-killing form of the event, in which the aim is only to dodge the charging bull in the arena.

Opposition to bullfighting is growing in Peru, where one poll found 80 percent of Lima's citizens to be against it. In 2011, Peru's minister of culture, Susana Baca stated that she opposed it. However, other Peruvians say bullfighting is a treasured cultural and artistic heritage and should be protected.

INTERNET LINKS

www.huffingtonpost.com/levi-novey/the-twisted-temptations-o_b_472989.html

An American reporter writes of her mixed emotions on attending a bullfight in Peru.

latincorrespondent.com/2014/10/great-economic-equalizer-peru-cockfighting

This article shines a light on cockfighting in Peru, with high-quality photos.

www.nytimes.com/2008/05/04/travel/04peru.html?pagewanted=all&_r=2&

This article is about the surfing "frenzy" that has swept Peru in recent years.

www.thesurfingsite.com/Surf-Spots-Peru.html

A quick overview of surfing in Peru is offered on this site.

FESTIVALS

A masked dancer performs in the 2015 *Virgen de la Candelaria* parade in Lima.

12

M

OST CULTURES OF THE WORLD observe certain special days with joy, music, dancing, and food. Latin American countries put on particularly colorful celebrations. The word *fiesta* is Spanish for "feast" and a fiesta day is often a holiday associated with a religious event. Even those observances that include solemn prayer and sacred rituals have a festive side as well. Church bells ring, fireworks explode, processions begin and end, and the eating and drinking never stop.

Today fiestas are held not only to commemorate religious events but also to mark ethnic-specific or national occasions. The most important national holidays are the Day of National Honor on October 9 and the Independence Days on July 28 and 29. They are occasions for speeches and military parades and a chance for local politicians to Campaign for upcoming elections.

Church festivals, on the other hand, are bright, energetic events, and far more popular. The Holy Week processions at Ayacucho, for example, attract people from all over the world.

The fiesta is an opportunity to bring color and laughter into lives that are often a hard struggle for existence. Whether the celebration is

Both Peru and Bolivia claim to be the true home of the ancient Andean ritual *La Diablada*, or "Devil's Dance." In 2009, Peru's candidate to the Miss Universe beauty pageant wore a La Diablada costume in the national costume competition. Bolivia immediately protested, saying the dance originated in Oruro, Bolivia, and that Miss Peru was impinging on its national brand and threatening its tourism industry.

An Andean man wears a richly decorated festival costume.

Christian, native, or a blend of African, Spanish, and Incan rituals, the fiesta is there to be enjoyed by everyone.

Each festival occurs only once a year, and because of this, it is eagerly awaited and anticipated by all. It is a day for the whole community to take part in and look forward to, a day when the poverty and hard work of everyday life are momentarily forgotten. It is therefore not surprising that each festival is celebrated in such high spirits.

COMMUNITY FIESTAS

Nearly every community in Peru has its own saint or patron figure, who is often very significant to local people. In the mountains and in small villages, their particular patron saint's day is both a splendid occasion and a well-earned holiday. The early Spanish missionaries, who were eager to get rid of the Incan religion, chose a saint's day that coincided with the most important pagan festival in each village, town, and city. This enabled them to change the pagan festival into an event of Christian significance.

A special type of fiesta is known as the *feria* (FAY-ree-ah), which means fair or market in Spanish. The feria usually falls on a weekday when no festival occurs. There is a solemn reason for feast days, but the feria is mainly for entertainment, although the local priest will often say Mass.

Religious festivals generally include a great fair or market, as well as fireworks, bullfights, communal dancing with the people in traditional dress, roast pig, and lots of chicha, a corn-based beer. Special masses are often said, sometimes combined with a procession that includes carrying a saint's statue or other holy images. Market days frequently coincide with fiestas, allowing local vendors to sell their wares to a large crowd.

Some of the most elaborate and colorful festivals are those belonging to the native peoples and the minority groups of blacks, Chinese, and Japanese who populate Peru. The September fiesta in Trujillo combines Andalusian,

CALENDAR OF FESTIVALS

January 1	New Year's Day
January 6	Epiphany
February	(First two weeks) Candlemas Festival, Fiesta de la Virgen de la Candelaria (Puno)
February-/March . . .	Carnival
March/April	Semana Santa (Holy Week), Easter
May 1	Labor Day
June	(Ninth Thursday after Easter) Corpus Christi
June 24	Inti Raymi in Cuzco Day
June 29	Saints Peter and Paul Day
July 28–29	Independence Days
August 15	Feast of the Assumption
August 30	Santa Rosa de Lima (Saint Rose of Lima) Festival, patron saint of Peru
October 8	Battle of Angamos Day
October 18	Lord of the Miracles in Lima
November 1	All Saints' Day
December 8	Feast of the Immaculate Conception
December 25	Christmas

African, and native music with skillful dancing. These dances are performed in peñas all over the country, but rarely are they performed as well as they are in Trujillo.

FIESTAS IN CUZCO

Cuzco, the city in the Andes that was once the capital of the Inca Empire, has an important fiesta occurring nearly every month. One of the oldest fiestas originated on March 31, 1650, when Cuzco was shattered by a major

Folk dancers perform in the Plaza de Armas in Cuzco for Holy Week festivities.

earthquake. A small statue known as Nuestro Señor de los Temblores (NWAY-stro say-NYOR day los taym-BLOH-rays), or "Our Lord of the Earthquakes," was taken out and paraded around the city. The people believed this saved them from further destruction. Every year since then, on the first Monday of Holy Week, this statue of Christ, known to the natives as Taitacha (tye-TAH-chah), meaning "Little Father," is carried on a three-hour circuit of Cuzco.

Corpus Christi occurs on the Thursday after Trinity Sunday. The day before this, thirteen statues of saints are taken from their respective churches in the suburbs or barrios of Cuzco. They are paraded on enormous litters, each carried by twenty to forty men and led by brass bands and parishioners who carry banners and candles and are followed by praying devotees. On Corpus Christi, the Plaza de Armas is filled with the faithful, some of whom come hundreds of miles to be there. Large altars decorated with flowers, mirrors, crosses—and images of the sun, remnants of Incan heritage—are erected on three sides of the plaza.

After High Mass the statues are paraded around the plaza on their litters until each has "bowed" to all the others. These litters can weigh up to a ton because of their gold and silver decorations. The litter is followed by other parishioners in brightly colored festival clothes and by musicians. Sometimes old women sing hymns in Quechua.

CARNIVAL

Carnavales (kar-nah-VAH-lays) is a great, joyous explosion celebrated throughout Peru. The word *carnival* comes from the Latin *carne vale*, which means "farewell to the flesh." Carnival is the last opportunity for people to drink, dance, and be merry before the fasting period of Lent.

The Quechua term for Carnavales is *jatum pujllay* (ja-TUM POOJ-lay), or "the great game." This originates from the native tradition of rounding up wild game for presentation to the parish priest and the mayor, who in return provided chicha and coca leaves. Today, because game is less plentiful, lambs and farm animals are usually offered. The offering of the animals is a fertility rite going back to Incan days, when the Incas gave offerings and sacrifices to their gods in anticipation of a good harvest. The idea of fertility survives today, as Carnival is still regarded by many as the best opportunity for meeting or courting future husbands and wives.

INTI RAYMI

Inti Raymi (Father Sun) or Festival of the Sun, on June 24, is the Incan celebration of the winter solstice, when the sun is farthest from the earth, and is dedicated to prayers for the return of the sun. The Incas believed that the sun regulates the universe and controls the lives of plants, animals, and people. Many modern natives still believe that the sun and moon are gods capable of punishing or helping people. Because the saint's day for Saint John the Baptist falls on June 24, the Spanish simply converted the ancient festival into a Christian one. Remnants of the original Incan festival still survive: fires left burning throughout the night of June 23 are not in praise of Saint John, but to bring back the sun after the longest night of the year.

The Inti Raymi of today was recreated in the 1940s based on eyewitness reports that the early colonists recorded. Before the ceremony, the festival's

DEVIL DANCERS IN PUNO

The department of Puno is located in the densely populated, poor, and southernmost part of Peru, bordering Lake Titicaca and Bolivia. It is the folk center of Peru and boasts a wide range of handicrafts, legends, costumes, and dances. More than three hundred ethnic dances are performed there, some of which are rarely seen by outsiders. The dances are usually reserved for the annual fiestas, especially church festivals, although they date from preconquest days. Many of them revolve around the agricultural life of the people and celebrate planting and harvest times.

Dancers wear elaborately embroidered costumes. These are extremely rich and ornate and are often the most expensive single item the family owns. Besides traditional indigenous attire with bowler hats and whirling skirts, the costumes also include grotesque masks, sequined uniforms, and animal costumes—all in bright colors.

The Diablada (dee-ah-BLAH-dah), or "Dance of the Devil" is traditionally performed during the feast of the Virgin of Candelaria, or Candlemas. Masked dancers compete fiercely to outdo each other in the dance, which symbolizes the victory of good over evil. The dancers gesticulate and contort their bodies into horrible positions and frighten the children. This dance probably dates to pre-Incan civilizations, but now features a costumed St. Michael imposing his will over a vast number of dancing devils. Besides symbolizing the fight between good and evil, it's also seen as a historical allegory of the native people's conversion to Christianity.

emperor and queen of all the Incas are chosen, and are carried through the streets on ornate thrones. A grand procession heads to Sacsayhuamán, the massive Inca fortress on the outskirts of Cuzco where the main ceremony takes place. Traditionally dressed dancers recreate an ancient battle that ended in victory. The pageant begins with a ceremonial relighting of the fires, which is symbolic of the return of the emperor and the Incas. People also burn their old clothes to symbolize an end to poverty, while marking the year's harvest and the beginning of the new year. A llama is sacrificed to the sun (but not killed), and the music and dancing go on for hours. The celebration continues through the rest of the week.

Girls dance at the Inti Raymi festival in Cuzco.

INTERNET LINKS

www.go2peru.com/peru_guide/cuzco/cuzco_feasts.htm
This is an overview of the feasts and festivals in Cuzco.

www.lonelyplanet.com/peru/cuzco/travel-tips-and-articles/77190
"Inti Raymi: a guide to the Incan Festival of the Sun in Peru" is found here.

www.peruthisweek.com/travel-inti-raymi-cuscos-biggest-festival-honoring-the-inca-sun-god-105487
Good photos are included in this article about Inti Raymi.

FOOD

A chef poses with his assistants in a restaurant kitchen in Lima.

13

PERUVIAN CUISINE IS ENJOYING A relatively newfound fame on the world's gastronomic stage, though the fare itself is not new. A nation's cookery reflects its natural setting, of course, but also its history and demographics. Peru's cuisine, therefore, began with the Incan and indigenous Andean ways with local foods, and, with the arrival of new peoples over time, grew into the unique fusion of culinary cultures that it is today. The country's varied climate and geography have produced the most extensive and assorted menu in South America. Lima, where Peruvian chefs have been taking this mixed cuisine to new heights, is now being called "a culinary powerhouse."

Specializing in spicy food, modern Peru has many local delicacies ranging from seafood on the coast to old Incan recipes such as roast guinea pig in peanut sauce. But the staples on which most of the population survive are still peppers, potatoes, and grains.

Yellow-hued Inca Kola is a soft drink that was created in Peru in 1935 by a British immigrant. Its flavor is sometimes compared to bubblegum or cream soda. Drinking Inca Kola is a matter of national pride and patriotism in Peru, where it is a national icon. Although the Coca-Cola Company bought the trademark for distribution outside of Peru, the drink has not proved popular internationally.

POTATOES, CORN, AND PEPPERS

Because the coast is too arid to grow many crops and the Amazon jungle is too densely forested to be cultivated, the majority of the crops come from the highlands. Potatoes are indigenous to the Andes and were exported from the highland regions to Europe and the rest of the Americas beginning in the sixteenth century. There are more than two hundred varieties, some completely unknown outside the Andes. A farmer with a small plot of land may plant up to three dozen different varieties in one field.

Some potatoes grow at altitudes of 8,000 feet (2,450 m) and higher, having adapted to that height and become frost resistant. People in the highlands freeze-dry their potato crop to ensure that food is available later in the season. The potatoes are frozen on the ground at night when the temperature is below zero and then thawed out the next day as the sun warms the air; they are then frozen again that night. This process continues until they are completely dehydrated. The potato becomes dry and cardboardlike. It is then stored and can be kept for up to four years. These potatoes, called *chuño* (choonyo) and *moraya* (more-I-ya), are popular in stews in the Andes, where they are cooked like any other vegetable.

Tunta, also called white chuño or moraya, is a freeze-dried potato made in the Andes.

Corn comes in as many varieties as the potato and was regarded as sacred by the indigenous peoples. It was used for bartering and as a form of currency, as well as for food.

Hot peppers, found in many varieties, are lavishly used in everything from fish to soups. Marketplaces become a dazzling display of color as enormous baskets full of peppers in sun-yellow, flaming orange, fiery red, and bright green are sold and bought. On the coast, where fish is common in the diet, sauces of onions and peppers are served in side bowls as condiments or heaped straight onto the meal. In the Amazon area, food is a little less spicy, but people there still dip vegetables in pepper sauces. It is in the highland areas that the *picante* (pee-KAHN-tay) or spicy form of cooking reaches an art form. Dishes are often laid out in degrees of spiciness according to the chili pepper used, ranging from bland to volcanic.

South American natives originally grew five different types of pepper, which gradually spread to Central America, Mexico, and the Caribbean. They were mistakenly called peppers by early Spanish explorers looking for black pepper. They found the natives were accustomed to eating peppers at every meal and soon began to export them to Europe, Africa, and Asia. In India, peppers became a staple in cooking.

TRADITIONAL CUISINE

Local dishes are often called *criolla*, or Creole, meaning they are a mixture of Spanish and indigenous cuisines. *A la criolla* also refers to spicy foods. Many cultures have contributed to Peruvian cuisine: slaves from the West Indies and Africa, Polynesian slaves from the Pacific Islands, Chinese and Japanese immigrants—and, of course, the Spanish and the native peoples.

Piqueo (pee-KAY-oh), or appetizers, are a specialty of Peru. The servings are frequently so large that there is little room for the main course. A favorite piqueo is Arequipa-style potatoes, or *Ocopas Arequipeña*. These are potatoes boiled, sliced, and served with a peanut, cheese, and chili sauce. Most appetizers are dips, and you can have many varieties at one sitting.

Anticuchos (an-tee-KOO-chohs) are also favorites. They are skewers of beef heart with hot peppers and seasoning barbecued over glowing coals. This dish is usually available from street vendors. *Causa a la Limeña* (COW-sah ah lah lee-MAY-nyah) is made from yellow potatoes, olives, onions, boiled eggs, peppers, prawns, and cheese.

Smoked fish is popular, especially smoked trout from the highlands. In the Pachamanca style of cooking, meat and frequently fish are cooked by wrapping them in leaves, usually banana, and steaming them beneath layers of earth and charcoal.

A platter of anticuchos, or skewered grilled beef heart, also includes boiled potato and white corn.

One of the best desserts is *mazamorra morada* (mah-zah-MOH-rah moh-RAH-dah), which is a sweet casserole made from pineapples, peaches, apples, dried fruit, quinces, sugar, and purple corn. It is served hot and sprinkled with cinnamon.

REGIONAL DELICACIES

Authentic Peruvian cuisine is more likely to be served in the highlands. Dishes include *rocoto relleno* (roh-COH-toh ray-YAY-noh), spicy bell peppers

Rocoto relleno is a stuffed pepper filled with meat and cheese.

stuffed with ground beef and vegetables; *chicharrones* (chee-chah-ROH-nays), deep-fried chunks of pork rib called *chancho* or chicken called *gallina*; *choclo con queso* (CHOH-cloh kon KAY-so), corn on the cob with cheese; and the obligatory *tamales*, cornmeal and meat or beans cooked in corn husks.

In the Amazon basin, people eat *farina*, a dish made from yucca, a plant similar to the potato. This is eaten fried or mixed with lemonade. In the markets, children sell hot *pan de arroz* (pahn day ah-ROHZ), a bread made from rice flour, yucca, and butter that takes three days to prepare. Some regional specialities include *juanes* (HWAH-nays), which is fish or chicken steamed in a banana leaf with rice or yucca, and *chocann* (CHOH-can), a soup of fish chunks flavored with cilantro. Fish dishes are popular, and the Amazon River provides everything from the small flesh-eating piranhas to the huge *paiches* (PIE-chays).

On the coast and in the desert regions, food is prepared in the same hearty manner as in the highlands, but with fish, chicken, or goat instead of beef. A favorite dish is roast kid cooked with chicha and served with beans and rice. But the best coastal dishes are those containing seafood. Ceviche (often spelled *cebiche* in Peru) or marinated raw whitefish, is perhaps Peru's most popular dish internationally. The raw fish is "cooked" in an acid, typically lime juice, with Andean chili peppers and onions.

DINING OUT

In most villages local restaurants called *picanterías* (literally "spicy places" because of the use of peppers) orquintas, country houses, serve typical dishes of the area. Most of the *picanterías* are open only two or three days a week, but because there are so many, one at least is always open. Live music is often played, and they are the social center of many communities. Quintas provide the same service in the suburbs.

Restaurants in Ollantaytambo attract hungry diners in this tourist town.

Another popular type of restaurant and one that shows Peru's ethnic diversity is the *chifas* (CHEE-fahs), or Chinese restaurants, that dot the coastal towns, making noodles part of the staple diet in some parts of Peru. Of a more basic nature are taverns called *chicherías* (chee-cha-REE-ahs), named after the Andean speciality chicha, the corn beer. They also serve meals and snacks.

Peruvian streets are often filled with vendors selling shish kebabs and fish—in fact, anything that is portable and edible. Generally, Peruvians have a very sweet tooth and indulge in the many desserts sold on the streets, like *churro* (CHOO-roh), a deep-fried tube of pastry filled with custard or, in the summer, cones of crushed ice flavored with fruit syrups, which are available on virtually every street corner.

DRINKS

Tap water in South America is not completely safe. Although it may come from a chlorination or filtration plant, the pipes that carry it to the tap may be old, cracked, or contain dirt. Only the elite and middle class drink bottled water, frequently the carbonated kind.

Tea is usually served with lemon and sugar. Peru grows its own coffee, but its coffee lacks the excellence of that grown in neighboring Colombia.

In many parts of the world, guinea pigs are kept as pets. In Peru, however, the cuddly companion is a staple food for the locals. About sixty-five million guinea pigs are consumed in Peru every year—often fried, roasted, or grilled over charcoal, and eaten with rice, potatoes, and salad. Said to taste like rabbit, it is also served in a stew in which the meat is marinated in beer before being cooked.

This well-loved Peruvian dish, known as cuy, *dates back to Incan times, when the commoners would dry out guinea pig skin, and use it in soups and stews. Every July the Incas would sacrifice one thousand guinea pigs along with one hundred llamas, to protect their crops from droughts and floods. Since then, farmers have bred the rodents for food. They are a vital source of protein for rural dwellers, and are used in traditional Andean medicine. Curanderos or spiritual healers still use them to diagnose illnesses.*

In 2004 Peruvian scientists introduced a new breed of "super" guinea pig, which is almost twice the normal size at 2.5 pounds (1.1 kg). Low in fat and cholesterol, it took more than thirty years to develop and is said to be meatier, tastier, and richer in protein than its precursor. Up to one thousand of these are exported weekly to the United States, Japan, and Europe, catering largely to the Peruvian expatriate and immigrant communities.

A traditional method of making coffee is to boil it for hours until only a thick, dark syrup, called *essencia* remains. This is poured into cruets, which are small glass bottles used for holding liquids, and diluted with hot milk or water. Nowadays instant coffee mix is more common.

Besides many of the usual varieties of soft drinks, or *gaseosas* (gah-say-OH-sas), sold in the United States, Peru also has its own varieties, which are very sweet. A local favorite is Inca Kola, a gold-colored, lemon verbena flavored soda. Fruit juices are common and come in many exotic flavors: blackberry, passion fruit, and watermelon, to name but a few.

Most adults, especially in rural areas, drink chicha. This beer is made by fermenting corn or quinoa (a plant with starchy seeds). Its thick, off-white appearance looks like soup and the taste is acquired. Some of the recipes date back to the Incas. A red or white bunch of flowers or a plastic bag on a pole is left outside a house to indicate that chicha is for sale there. Peru's national drink, *pisco*, a clear wine made of white grapes, gets its name from the city of Pisco in southern Peru.

INTERNET LINKS

www.npr.org/sections/thesalt/2013/03/12/174105739/from-pets-to-plates-why-more-people-are-eating-guinea-pigs
This article is about the growing popularity of eating guinea pigs.

www.npr.org/sections/thesalt/2014/09/17/349038162/mistura-food-fest-gives-peruvian-cuisine-a-chance-to-shine
This article is about a Peruvian food festival.

www.seriouseats.com/2015/06/essential-peruvian-cuisine.html
Ten top Peruvian dishes with photos.

southamericanfood.about.com/od/exploresouthamericanfood/tp/PeruvianFood.htm
This is a list of popular Peruvian dishes with links to recipes.

PAPA A LA HUANCAÍNA (HUANCAYO-STYLE POTATOES)

4 medium potatoes, such Yukon Gold

1 clove garlic, chopped

¼ pound (115 grams) queso fresco or feta cheese, crumbled; alternatively, use cottage cheese or cream cheese

1 5-ounce (147 mL) can evaporated milk

1 ½ tablespoon bottled ají amarillo paste; alternatively, use 1 chopped and seeded jalapeno pepper

2 saltine crackers (optional)

1 tablespoon chopped onion

1 tablespoon olive oil

4 or 5 large lettuce leaves, such as Bibb or romaine, or enough to line a platter

2 hard boiled eggs, peeled and sliced

Garnish: chopped parsley, chopped pitted black Botija Peruvian or Kalamata olives.

Cover potatoes with water in a medium pot and season well with salt. Simmer, covered, until just cooked through, about 20 minutes. Drain and cool, and then peel.

Mince garlic and mash to a paste with a pinch of salt. Place in a blender with the remaining ingredients (not the lettuce, eggs, or garnishes) and blend until smooth. Sauce should be pourable, but thicker than heavy cream. If necessary, thin with milk. Season with salt.

Cut potatoes crosswise into ¼-inch- (6 mm) thick slices.

Line a platter with the lettuce leaves and arrange the sliced potatoes on top. Pour the sauce over the potatoes. Garnish with slices of hard-boiled egg, olives, and chopped parsley. Serve chilled or at room temperature.

LOMO SALTADO (PERUVIAN BEEF STIR-FRY)

16 ounces (500 grams) frozen French fries

2 tablespoons balsamic vinegar

1 Tbsp soy sauce

1 teaspoon aji amarillo (yellow hot pepper)
   paste

1 tsp brown sugar

1 lb. (500g) beef tenderloin or sirloin, thinly
   sliced

Salt, pepper

3 Tbsp vegetable oil (not olive oil)

2 red onions, thinly sliced

2 mild yellow, orange, or red peppers,
   seeded and sliced into strips

2 tsp minced garlic

2 plum tomatoes, thickly sliced

Fresh chopped cilantro

Lime juice

White rice, served on the side

Prepare French fried potatoes according to package directions. In a small bowl, mix together vinegar, soy sauce, pepper paste, and sugar. Set aside. Season the meat with salt and pepper.

Heat a wok or large sauté pan until very hot. Swirl oil; and add the meat a few slices at a time, so as not to crowd the pan, and cook until brown on both sides, about 3 minutes. Set aside.

Add onion and peppers, and stir fry about 2 or 3 minutes. Add garlic, and stir fry about 30 seconds more. Add tomatoes and vinegar mixture. Mix together just until warmed through. Don't let tomatoes get mushy. Stir in cooked potatoes.

Sprinkle with fresh chopped cilantro and a dash of lime juice. Serve with rice.

Serves 4.

A   **B**   **C**   **D**

Equator

ECUADOR

COLOMBIA

1

Capital city
Major town
Mountain peak
Ancient site

Feet   Meters
16,500   5,000
9,900   3,000
6,600   2,000
3,300   1,000
1,650   500
660   200
0   0

TUMBES
Talara
Sullana
Piura · Chulucanas
PIURA

AMAZONAS

Tigre

L O R E T O

Iquitos

Nauta

Amazon

Marañón

Huallaga

N

2

LAMBAYEQUE
Chiclayo

CAJAMARCA

Cajamarca

SAN MARTÍN

Ucayali

B R A Z I L

Chan Chan
Trujillo
LA LIBERTAD

P
e
r
u

3

Chimbote

Mount Huascarán
(22,205 ft / 6,765m)
▲

ANCASH

HUÁNUCO
Huánuco

PASCO

UCAYALI

Urubamba

C
u
r
r
e
n
t

JUNÍN

Callao
LIMA
LIMA

Huancayo

**MADRE DE
DIOS**

Madre de Dios

4

HUANCAVELICA

Chincha
Island
Pisco

ICA
Nazca

Apurímac

Machu Picchu
Ruins
■ **CUZCO**

Chincheros
Cuzco

AYACUCHO

APURÍMAC

BOLIVIA

PUNO

**PACIFIC
OCEAN**

AREQUIPA

Matarani
Mollendo

Arequipa

El Misti
▲

Lake
Titicaca
Puno

MOQUEGUA

5

TACNA
Tacna

CHILE

MAP OF PERU

Amazon (river),
C2
Ancash (region),
A3—B3
Apurimac
(region), B4—
C4
Arequipa, C5
Ayacucho
(region), B4—
B5, C4—C5

Bolivia, C4—C5,
D3—D5
Brazil, C2—C4,
D1—
D4

Cajamarca, A3
Callao, B4
Chan Chan, A3
Chiclayo, A2
Chile, C5—D5
Chimbote, A3
Chincheros, B4
Chincha Island,
B4

Chulucanas, A2
Colombia, B1,
C1—C2
Cuzco, C4

Ecuador, A1—
A2, B1
El Misti, C5

Huancavelica
(region), B4
Huancayo, B4
Huánuco
(region), B3

Ica (region), B4
Iquitos, C2

Junín (region),
B3—B4, C4

La Libertad
(region), A3—
B3
Lake Titicaca,
C5
Lima, B4

Machu Picchu
Ruins, C4
Madre de Dios
(region), C3—
C4
Marañón
(river), B2
Matarani, C5
Mollendo, C5
Mount
Huascarán,
B3
Nauta (city), C2
Nazca, B4

Pasco (region),
B3—B4
Pisco, B4
Piura, A2
Puno, C5

Sullana, A2

Tacna, C5
Talara, A2
Tigre (river),
B1—B2

Trujillo, A3

Urubamba
(river), C3—
C4

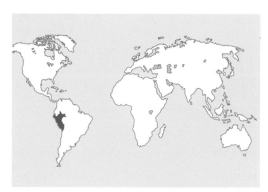

133

ECONOMIC PERU

Natural Resources

- **Cu** Copper
- Fish
- Gold
- Guano
- Hydroelectricity
- Lead and zinc
- Natural Gas
- Petroleum
- **Ag** Silver
- Timber

Services

- Airport
- Port
- Tourism

Manufacturing

- Petroleum Refinery
- Steel
- Textiles

Agriculture

- Coffee
- Corn
- Cotton
- Rice
- Sugarcane
- Vineyards
- Wool

ABOUT THE ECONOMY

GROSS DOMESTIC PRODUCT (GDP)
$202.6 billion (2014)

GDP BY SECTORS
Services 57.5 percent; industry 35.5 percent; agriculture 7 percent (2014)

GDP PER CAPITA
$11,900 (2014)

NATURAL RESOURCES
Iron, copper, gold, silver, zinc, lead, fish, petroleum, natural gas, timber, coal, phosphate, potash, hydropower

AGRICULTURAL PRODUCTS
Artichokes, asparagus, avocados, blueberries, coffee, cocoa, cotton, sugarcane, rice, potatoes, corn, plantains, grapes, oranges, pineapples, guavas, bananas, apples, lemons, pears, coca, tomatoes, mangoes, barley, medicinal plants, quinoa, palm oil, marigold, onion, wheat, dry beans; poultry, beef, pork, dairy products; guinea pigs; fish

LAND USE
Agricultural land, 18.8 percent; forest, 53 percent; other, 28.2 percent (2011)

CURRENCY
Nuevo sol
USD 1 = 3.46 nuevo sol (PEN) (January 2016)

MAIN EXPORTS
copper, gold, lead, zinc, tin, iron ore, molybdenum, silver; crude petroleum and petroleum products, natural gas; coffee, asparagus and other vegetables, fruit, apparel and textiles, fishmeal, fish, chemicals, fabricated metal products and machinery, alloys

MAIN IMPORTS
petroleum and petroleum products, chemicals, plastics, machinery, vehicles, TV sets, power shovels, front-end loaders, telephones and telecommunication equipment, iron and steel, wheat, corn, soybean products, paper, cotton, vaccines and medicines

MAJOR EXPORT MARKETS
China, United States, Switzerland, Canada, Brazil, Japan (2014)

MAJOR IMPORT SUPPLIERS
China, United States, Brazil, Mexico, Ecuador (2014)

LABOR FORCE
16.55 million (2014)

LABOR FORCE BY SECTOR
Services 56.8 percent, industry 17.4 percent, agriculture 25.8 percent (2011)

UNEMPLOYMENT RATE
5.5 percent (2014 estimate)

POPULATION BELOW POVERTY LINE
25.8 percent (2012)

CULTURAL PERU

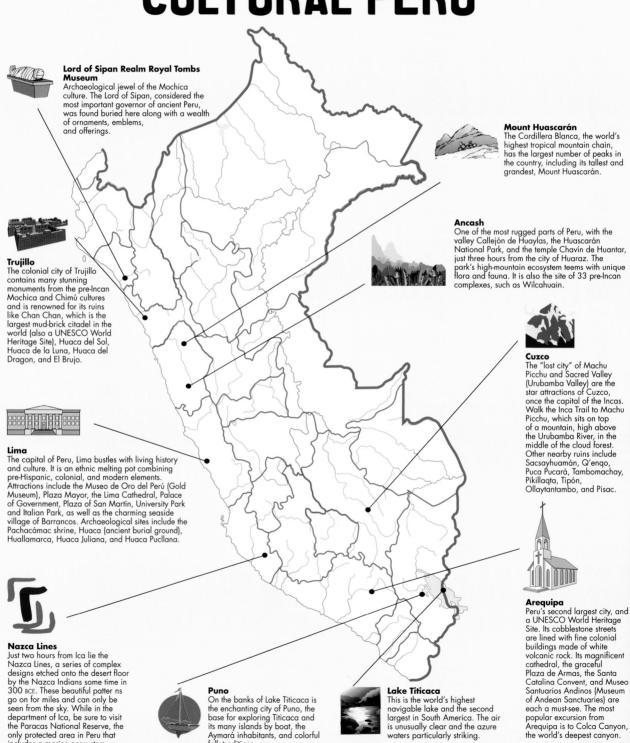

Lord of Sipan Realm Royal Tombs Museum
Archaeological jewel of the Mochica culture. The Lord of Sipan, considered the most important governor of ancient Peru, was found buried here along with a wealth of ornaments, emblems, and offerings.

Mount Huascarán
The Cordillera Blanca, the world's highest tropical mountain chain, has the largest number of peaks in the country, including its tallest and grandest, Mount Huascarán.

Ancash
One of the most rugged parts of Peru, with the valley Callejón de Huaylas, the Huascarán National Park, and the temple Chavín de Huantar, just three hours from the city of Huaraz. The park's high-mountain ecosystem teems with unique flora and fauna. It is also the site of 33 pre-Incan complexes, such as Wilcahuain.

Trujillo
The colonial city of Trujillo contains many stunning monuments from the pre-Incan Mochica and Chimú cultures and is renowned for its ruins like Chan Chan, which is the largest mud-brick citadel in the world (also a UNESCO World Heritage Site), Huaca del Sol, Huaca de la Luna, Huaca del Dragon, and El Brujo.

Cuzco
The "lost city" of Machu Picchu and Sacred Valley (Urubamba Valley) are the star attractions of Cuzco, once the capital of the Incas. Walk the Inca Trail to Machu Picchu, which sits on top of a mountain, high above the Urubamba River, in the middle of the cloud forest. Other nearby ruins include Sacsayhuamán, Q'enqo, Puca Pucará, Tambomachay, Pikillaqta, Tipón, Ollaytantambo, and Pisac.

Lima
The capital of Peru, Lima bustles with living history and culture. It is an ethnic melting pot combining pre-Hispanic, colonial, and modern elements. Attractions include the Museo de Oro del Perú (Gold Museum), Plaza Mayor, the Lima Cathedral, Palace of Government, Plaza of San Martín, University Park and Italian Park, as well as the charming seaside village of Barrancos. Archaeological sites include the Pachacámac shrine, Huaca (ancient burial ground), Huallamarca, Huaca Juliana, and Huaca Pucllana.

Arequipa
Peru's second largest city, and a UNESCO World Heritage Site. Its cobblestone streets are lined with fine colonial buildings made of white volcanic rock. Its magnificent cathedral, the graceful Plaza de Armas, the Santa Catalina Convent, and Museo Santuarios Andinos (Museum of Andean Sanctuaries) are each a must-see. The most popular excursion from Arequipa is to Colca Canyon, the world's deepest canyon.

Nazca Lines
Just two hours from Ica lie the Nazca Lines, a series of complex designs etched onto the desert floor by the Nazca Indians some time in 300 BCE. These beautiful patter ns go on for miles and can only be seen from the sky. While in the department of Ica, be sure to visit the Paracas National Reserve, the only protected area in Peru that includes a marine ecosystem.

Puno
On the banks of Lake Titicaca is the enchanting city of Puno, the base for exploring Titicaca and its many islands by boat, the Aymará inhabitants, and colorful folk traditions.

Lake Titicaca
This is the world's highest navigable lake and the second largest in South America. The air is unusually clear and the azure waters particularly striking.

OFFICIAL NAME
Republic of Peru

NATIONAL FLAG
Three vertical red-white-red stripes, with a coat of arms in the middle. This contains a shield featuring a vicuña, a cinchona tree, and a yellow cornucopia spilling with gold coins, all framed by a green wreath.

CAPITAL
Lima

INDEPENDENCE
July 28, 1821

MAJOR CITIES
Lima, Arequipa, Callao, Trujillo, Chiclayo, Piura

DEPARTMENTS
Amazonas, Ancash, Apurímac, Arequipa, Ayacucho, Cajamarca, Callao, Cuzco, Huancavelica, Huánuco, Ica, Junín, La Libertad, Lambayeque, Lima, Loreto, Madre de Dios, Moquegua, Pasco, Piura, Puno, San Martín, Tacna, Tumbes and Ucayali

POPULATION
30,445,000 (2015)

MAIN GEOGRAPHIC REGIONS
Costa (western coastal region);
Sierra (central Andes region);
Selva (eastern rain forest region)

HIGHEST POINT
Mount Huascarán at 22,205 feet (6,765 m)

ETHNIC GROUPS
Indigenous 45 percent, mestizo 37 percent, European 15 percent, African, Japanese, Chinese and others 3 percent (2005 estimate)

OFFICIAL LANGUAGES
Spanish and Quechua

LITERACY
94.5 percent (2015)

RELIGION
Roman Catholic, 81.3 percent; Evangelical, 12.5 percent; other, 3.3 percent; none, 2.9 percent (2007)

LIFE EXPECTANCY
73.5 years (2015)

TIMELINE

IN PERU	IN THE WORLD
40,000–15,000 BCE First Peruvians descended from nomadic tribes during the last Ice Age.	
5000 BCE Cotton is first cultivated in Peru.	**753** BCE Rome is founded.
300 BCE–CE 700 Rise of Nazca cultures; Nazca Lines drawn.	**116–117** CE The Roman Empire reaches its greatest extent.
300 CE Burial of Mochican leader, Lord of Sipán.	**600** CE Height of Mayan civilization.
	1000 The Chinese perfect gunpowder and begin to use it in warfare.
1200 Manco Cápac becomes the first Incan emperor of the Inca Empire.	
1438–1493 Reign of Pachacútec; Sacsayhuamán and Machu Picchu are built.	**1530** Beginning of transatlantic slave trade.
1527–1533 Division of the Incan empire sparks civil war. Atahualpa gains control of the entire empire but is captured by Spanish conquistador, Francisco Pizarro and assassinated by Spaniards.	
1535 Pizarro makes Lima the capital of the Viceroyalty of Peru.	**1558–1603** Reign of Elizabeth I of England
1572 Tupac Amaru, the last Incan emperor, is captured and executed.	**1620** Pilgrims sail the *Mayflower* to America.
	1776 US Declaration of Independence.
	1789–1799 The French Revolution.
1824 Peru defeats Spain and becomes last Latin American colony to gain independence.	**1861–1865** The US Civil War.
	1869 The Suez Canal is opened.
1879–1883 Peru defeated in War of the Pacific and loses southern territory to Chile.	

IN PERU	IN THE WORLD
	• **1914–1919** World War I.
1941 •	• **1939–1945** World War II.
Peru gains the northern Amazon in the war against Ecuador.	
	• **1966–1969** The Chinese Cultural Revolution.
1980 •	
Maoist terrorist group Sendero Luminoso (Shining Path) and Tupac Amaru Revolutionary Movement guerrillas start civil war.	
1985–1988 •	
President Alan García Pérez's policies cause hyperinflation and Peru seeks assistance from the International Monetary Fund.	• **1986** Nuclear power disaster at Chernobyl in Ukraine.
1990 •	
Alberto Fujimori becomes president and institutes severe market reforms.	• **1991** Break-up of the Soviet Union.
1997 •	• **1997** Hong Kong is returned to China.
El Niño—the worst of the century—causes severe drought in Peru.	
2000–2005 •	• **2001** Terrorists crash planes in New York, Washington, DC, and Pennsylvania.
Fujimori wins a third five-year term but political corruption forces him into exile. Alejandro Toledo is Peru's first president of native origin but his term is mired in crisis.	• **2003** War in Iraq.
2006 •	
Alan García wins the second round of the Peruvian presidential elections.	• **2008** United States elects first African American president, Barack Obama.
2009 •	
Alberto Fujimori is sentenced and sent to prison.	
	• **2015** Islamist terrorists attack Paris.
2016 •	• **2016** United States presidential elections take place.
Ollanta Humala steps down at the end of his term and new presidential elections are held.	

GLOSSARY

ají (a-HE)
A South American chili varying in color from orange-red to yellow or brown.

barrio (BAH-ree-oh)
District, neighborhood, or suburb.

chicha (CHEE-chah)
Beer made from fermented corn.

cholo (CHOH-loh)
Indigenous person trying to join mestizo society.

Creole (kre-ol)
Person of European descent born in Spanish America.

curandero (kur-ahn-DAIR-oh)
A spiritual healer, shaman, or folk doctor.

encomenderos (en-koh-men-DER-ohs)
Local village chiefs in colonial times.

encomienda (en-koh-MYEN-dah)
System instituted by the Spanish colonizers: land was given to a Spaniard, who had the right to force the natives living there to work.

hispanistas (ees-pan-EES-tahs)
Artists using a Spanish-derived style.

indigenistas (een-dee-hain-EES-tahs)
Artists using native subjects for their work.

machismo (mah-CHEES-moh)
Belief in male strength and superiority.

mestizo (mes-TEE-zoh)
Person of mixed Spanish and native origin.

picante (pee-KAHN-tay)
Spicy; a style of cooking spicy foods.

quipu (KEE-poo)
System of knotted string that Incas used for communication.

Selva
Amazon region east of the Andes.

Sendero Luminoso (sen-DER-oh loo-mee-NOH-soh)
"Shining Path," a guerrilla group.

shaman
Village healer providing herbal medicine.

Sierra
Mountainous Andes region running through the center of Peru.

FOR FURTHER INFORMATION

BOOKS

Adams, Mark. *Turn Right at Machu Picchu: Rediscovering the Lost City One Step at a Time*. New York: Plume, Penguin Group, 2012.

Cuadra, Morena and Morena Escardo. *The Everything Peru Cookbook*. Avon, Mass.: Adams Media, 2013.

DK Eyewitness Travel Guide: Peru. New York: Dorling Kindersley Publishing, 2014.

Mac Quarrie, Kim. *The Last Days of the Incas*. New York: Simon & Schuster, 2007

Zarate, Ricardo and Jenn Garbee. *The Fire of Peru: Recipes and Stories from My Peruvian Kitchen*. New York: Houghton Mifflin, 2015.

ONLINE

BBC News Peru Country Profile. news.bbc.co.uk/2/hi/americas/country_profiles/1224656.stm

CIA World Factbook. Peru. www.cia.gov/library/publications/the-world-factbook/geos/pe.html

Geographia. Peru. www.geographia.com/peru/index.htm

Living In Peru. www.peruthisweek.com

Lonely Planet. Peru. www.lonelyplanet.com/peru

My Peru. www.myperu.org

National Geographic. Peru Guide. travel.nationalgeographic.com/travel/countries/peru-guide

New York Times, The. Times Topics, Peru. topics.nytimes.com/top/news/international/countriesandterritories/peru/index.html

Perú, Official travel and tourism portal. www.peru.travel/en-us

Peruvian Times. www.peruviantimes.com

UNESCO World Heritage List. Peru. whc.unesco.org/en/statesparties/pe

FILMS

NOVA: Ghosts of Machu Picchu. PBS, 2010.

NOVA: Secrets of Lost Empires—Inca. PBS, 2006.

MUSIC

Peru: Andean Music of Life Work & Celebration, UNESCO, 2015

Traditional Music of Peru series, albums 1—8, Smithsonian Folkways, 1995—2002

BIBLIOGRAPHY

Araujo Herrera, Mariana. "The Asháninka: Illegal Logging Threatening Indigenous Rights and Sustainable Development in the Peruvian Amazon." Council on Hemispheric Affairs, September 29, 2015. http://www.coha.org/the-ashaninka-illegal-logging-threatening-indigenous-rights-and-sustainable-development-in-the-peruvian-amazon.

Associated Press. "Cocaine is winning the drug war in Peru." *New York Post*, October 14, 2015. http://nypost.com/2015/10/14/cocaine-is-winning-the-drug-war-in-peru.

BBC News. Timeline: Peru. http://news.bbc.co.uk/2/hi/americas/country_profiles/1224690.stm.

Bland, Alistair. "From Pets to Plates: Why More People Are Eating Guinea Pigs." NPR, April 2, 2013. http://www.npr.org/sections/thesalt/2013/03/12/174105739/from-pets-to-plates-why-more-people-are-eating-guinea-pigs.

Dube, Ryan. "Land Used for Coca Cultivation in Peru at 15-Year Low." *The Wall Street Journal*, July 15, 2015. http://www.wsj.com/articles/land-used-for-coca-cultivation-in-peru-at-15-year-low-1436981907.

Figueroa, Dante and Jonathan Arendt. "Current Constitutional Developments in Latin America." Globalex, June/July 2013. http://www.nyulawglobal.org/globalex/Constitutional_Developments_Latin_America1.html.

Goldenberg, Sonia. "Peru's Possible Prison Presidency." *The New York Times*, February 1, 2016. http://www.nytimes.com/2016/02/02/opinion/perus-possible-prison-presidency.html?ref=topics&_r=0.

Moffett, Matt and Robert Kozak. "In This Spat Between Bolivia and Peru, the Details Are in the Devils." *The Wall Street Journal*, August 21, 2009. http://www.wsj.com/articles/SB125081309502848049.

Novey, Levi and Barbara Drake. "The Twisted Temptations of Bullfighting in Peru." *The World Post*, May 25, 2010. http://www.huffingtonpost.com/levi-novey/the-twisted-temptations-o_b_472989.html.

Pashley, Alex. "In Peru, cockfighting is more than just a sport." *Latin Correspondent*, October 2, 2014. http://latincorrespondent.com/2014/10/great-economic-equalizer-peru-cockfighting

Peru Reports. http://perureports.com.

Pyper, Neil. "How Peru's drug trade is threatening its economic growth." The Conversation, July 28, 2015. http://theconversation.com/how-perus-drug-trade-is-threatening-its-economic-growth-45018.

Sullivan, Lynda. "Peru's Tia Maria Mining Conflict: Another Mega Imposition." Truthout, June 28, 2015. http://www.truth-out.org/news/item/31619-peru-s-tia-maria-mining-conflict-another-mega-imposition.

INDEX

INDEX